Central Statistics Office
An Phríomh-Oifig Staidrimh

D0551737

That was then, This is now

Change in Ireland, 1949-1999

A publication to mark the 50th anniversary of the Central Statistics Office

Edited by Adrian Redmond

Pn 8084   Price: £15.00   February 2000
€19.05

ISBN 0-7076-1934-3

Published by the Stationery Office, Dublin.

Designed and produced by the Central Statistics Office.

Contents

Introduction

This book uses official statistics from the Central Statistics Office and other sources to provide a synopsis of the development of the economy and society in Ireland over the last 50 years, from the founding of the CSO in 1949 to the dawn of the new millennium. It consists of articles written by CSO staff.

During World War II (or The Emergency as the war was called in Ireland), ordinary life was severely affected. There was widespread rationing, covering butter, margarine, bread, tea, flour, clothes, coal, firewood, gas and matches. There was a shortage of fuel for cooking and heating. As the war wore on, private motoring ceased to exist and horse-drawn vehicles were brought back into service. The hardship continued for some years after the war.

In 1949, life began to return to normal and most rationing ceased. But normal life in 1949 was very different from what it is today. The risk of death from tuberculosis and other infectious diseases was high. Very few people had telephones or cars. The radio was widespread, though the television had yet to be seen. Society was, by current standards, very conservative. Censorship was severe — George Orwell's 1984 was banned in 1949. There was little cohabitation, and births outside marriage were rare. Women, when they married, usually ceased working outside the home. We were a still a mainly rural society: only two-fifths of the population lived in towns of over 1,500.

The economy in 1949 was also recovering from the effects of the war. But while the economy grew by a healthy 5% in that year, it was followed by several years of relative stagnation. Emigration was very high (the population was still falling despite the high birth rate), we were importing far more than we were exporting, and families had to spend a high proportion of their income on food and clothing.

Irish society has changed dramatically during the past half century. We have, for example, become a mainly urban society: by 1996, 60% of the population lived in towns of over 1,500. Looking at the official statistics from various sources, we can track the emergence of major changes in society, such as the increasing participation by women in the labour force, the decline in the popularity of marriage and the rise in one-parent families, the greater use of the educational system, the increasing diversification of our religious beliefs, the state of the Irish language, the impact of television, the increasing use of the telephone, and the surge in crime in the 1960s and 1970s.

In the 1990s, Ireland's pace of social change accelerated. The influence of the Catholic Church waned further. Divorce was legalised. Contraceptives became freely available. Taboos were increasingly being broken: a more liberal view was taken of pornographic material and the tabloid press became more sensational. In many areas of life, women were achieving a status never obtained before. There were women Presidents, a woman member of the Supreme Court, and an increasing number of women members in the Dáil. The influx of foreigners from a wide range of countries made the society more cosmopolitan. In 1946, 3.3% of the population was born outside Ireland, and the vast majority of those came from the UK. The 1996 Census shows that 7% of the population were born outside the country, the biggest relative increase being for those born in countries other than the UK and the US.

In contrast to the economic situation in 1949, the economy is now strong and has been growing in recent years at an unprecedented rate. Inflation, after the high price increases of the 1970s and early 1980s, has fallen back to a low level. The trade balance has been reversed: we now export far more than we import. There has been a steady shift from agriculture to services and high-technology industry.

The rise in our creature comforts can be seen in the amount of electricity we consumed in our homes. In 1949, domestic consumption was less than 300 million units. This might seem a large number, but it was lower than the amount generated in that year by the turbines in the hydro-electric station at Ardnacrusha, which had started operating 20 years previously in 1929. (The country was so dependent on hydroelectricity that, during the drought in the summer of 1949, a system of quotas had to be introduced to control the household consumption of electricity.) Over the intervening years, our domestic consumption of electricity rose steadily. It passed the one billion level in 1963 and the 3 billion level in 1978. By 1997, it was close to 6 billion units and still rising strongly. Other signs of our increasing prosperity can be seen in rising house prices, congested roads, the shorter working week, increasing tourist numbers, and the influx of economic refugees.

During the past fifty years, the CSO has quite successfully informed the nation on the social, demographic and economic changes that have occurred over the period. For this, thanks is due to the dedicated staff of the Office and to the leadership of the successive Directors: Dr Roy Geary (1949-1957), Dr Donal McCarthy (1957-1967), and Tom Linehan (1967-1991). Statistics will have an increasingly important role to play in the new millennium as the country continues to develop and the information society gathers pace. The CSO is committed to meeting this challenge.

Donal Murphy
Director General

Changing Population Structure

Aidan Punch, Catherine Finneran

1

OVERALL TRENDS

The last 50 years have witnessed a population increase of over 670,000 persons. The most recent census, conducted in April 1996, recorded a population of over 3.6 million compared with less than 3 million as returned in the May 1946 census.

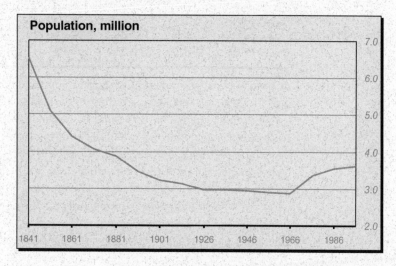

Population, million

To gain a fuller appreciation of recent population trends, it is necessary to view them over a longer period. As the graph shows, the population of the area comprising the Republic of Ireland was over 6.5 million in 1841. The deaths caused by the famine of 1846/47 as well as the large-scale emigration that followed in its wake and which continued through the second half of the 19th century resulted in a halving of the population by 1901. Further declines, albeit more modest compared with earlier periods, followed between 1901 and 1926. The population then stabilised at around 2.9 million for the next quarter of a century, before falling to a historical low point of 2.8 million in 1961. Apart from the slight decline experienced between 1986 and 1991, the direction of population change has since been firmly upward.

CAUSES OF POPULATION CHANGE SINCE 1946

The change in population between two periods is due to changes in the number of births and deaths as well as the difference between inward and outward migration. The table shows each of these components of population change on an annual average basis for each of the intercensal periods since 1946.

Annual average births, deaths and net migration (000)

Intercensal period	Births	Deaths	Natural increase	Net migration	Population change
1946-1951	66	40	26	-24	+1
1951-1956	63	36	27	-39	-12
1956-1961	61	34	26	-42	-16
1961-1966	63	33	29	-16	+13
1966-1971	63	33	30	-11	+19
1971-1979	69	33	35	+14	+49
1979-1981	73	33	40	-3	+38
1981-1986	67	33	34	-14	+19
1986-1991	56	32	24	-27	-3
1991-1996	50	31	18	+2	+20

In the earlier part of the period, net outward migration exceeded the natural increase in the population (births less deaths), resulting in the population declining to its 1961 low point. The main factor causing this fall was the high emigration that occurred during the 1950s. Births began to increase in the 1970s to reach a peak of 74,000 in 1980. During the same period migration turned from outward to inward with the result that the population grew by 465,000 in the ten-year period from 1971 to 1981. Net outward migration strengthened during the eighties and this resulted in a slight decline in overall population levels between 1986 and 1991. However, since then the fall in outward migration has given rise once more to population growth.

GEOGRAPHIC DISTRIBUTION

Ireland has changed from being a predominantly rural country to a more urbanised one during the course of the last 50 years. The 1946 population could be characterised as mainly rural with over 60% of persons living either in the countryside or in smaller towns and villages with a population of less than 1,500 persons. In contrast, over 58% of the population lived in urban areas in 1996, as revealed by the most recent census.

In the 50-year period 1946 to 1996, Leinster's population has grown from 1.3 million to over 1.9 million. The increase in population in the Munster area was far less pronounced (from 900,000 to just over 1 mil-

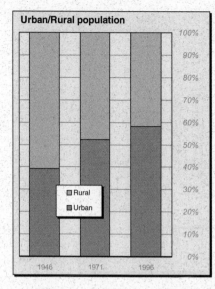

Urban/Rural population

□ Rural
■ Urban

1946   1971   1996

lion). Connacht and Ulster both experienced population declines in the same period. As a result, in proportionate terms, Leinster has continued to gain population share over the last 50 years from 43.4% in 1946 to 53% in 1996. This gain has been at the expense of the other three provinces, each of which experienced declining population shares at each census since 1946. Connacht and Ulster combined accounted for less than one in five of the population of the State in 1996, while Munster's share stood at 28.5%. This compares with shares of 26% and 31% respectively in 1946.

Dublin has been the major growth area in the course of the past 50 years with a population increase of two-thirds for the area comprising Dublin city and county combined. The population of Dublin city (or County Borough) increased from just over a half a million inhabitants in 1946 to 568,000 by 1971. However, the depopulation of the inner city area saw the population fall back to 482,000 in the most recent census. The number of persons in the Dublin county area — the 1996 equivalent is the Counties of Fingal, South Dublin and Dún Laoghaire/Rathdown — more than doubled in each of the 25 year periods 1946-71 and 1971-96, resulting in a population of 576,000 in 1996.

Population of cities and larger towns

	1946	1971	1996
Dublin city and county	636,200	852,200	1,058,300
Dublin city (excluding suburbs)	506,100	567,900	481,900
Dublin county	130,100	284,400	576,499
Cork city	89,900	134,400	180,000
Limerick city	43,000	63,000	79,100
Galway city	20,400	29,400	57,400
Waterford city	28,300	33,700	44,200
Dundalk	18,600	23,800	30,200
Bray	11,100	15,800	27,900
Drogheda	15,700	20,100	25,300
Swords	700	4,100	22,300

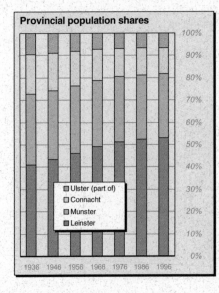

Provincial population shares

100%
90%
80%
70%
60%
50%
40%
30%
20%
10%
0%

□ Ulster (part of)
□ Connacht
□ Munster
□ Leinster

1936 1946 1956 1966 1976 1986 1996

The growth in the four remaining County Borough areas in the country including their suburbs, though less spectacular than in the case of Dublin, has still been impressive. The population of Galway nearly trebled in size during the 50-year period 1946-1996. Of the towns with a population of over 20,000 persons in 1996, Swords was the one to experience the most dramatic increase in population over the half century, from a little village with less than 1,000 inhabitants in 1946 to a large urban centre with over 22,000 persons in 1996. Many small towns and villages that existed as separate entities in 1946 have since been subsumed into larger urban areas. An example is Tallaght in South Dublin.

At the other extreme, the population of the islands off the coast of Ireland halved from 18,655 inhabitants in 1946 to 9,280 in 1996. There were five islands with a population of over 1,000 persons in 1946. These were Achill in County Mayo, Gorumna and Inishmore in County Galway, Aran in County Donegal, and Valencia in County Kerry. Between them, they accounted for just over a half of the island population in 1946. Fifty years later the same islands represented over two-thirds of the total island population, with the most populous island, Achill, having 2,718 inhabitants.

SEX RATIO

Overall, the number of males exceeded the number of females by almost 35,000 in 1946, corresponding to a sex ratio (number of males per 100 females) of 102.4. However, by 1996 the sex ratio had fallen to 98.6, reflecting a female excess of 25,000 in that year. The data classified by age group are given in the table.

Population by sex and age group

1946

Age	Males	Females	Males per 100 females
0-4	150,500	144,200	104.4
5-14	268,400	259,800	103.3
15-24	245,900	236,900	103.8
25-34	208,000	204,900	101.5
35-44	181,800	175,600	103.5
45-54	156,900	153,600	102.2
55-64	127,700	126,400	101.1
65-74	108,400	106,000	102.2
75-84	41,700	45,000	92.6
85 & over	5,500	7,700	71.6
Total	1,494,900	1,460,200	102.4

1996

Age	Males	Females	Males per 100 females
0-4	128,700	121,700	105.8
5-14	312,700	296,300	105.5
15-24	323,100	309,800	104.3
25-34	257,100	262,900	97.8
35-44	246,200	249,900	98.5
45-54	208,600	203,400	102.6
55-64	146,500	145,300	100.9
65-74	110,400	129,000	85.6
75-84	56,300	83,600	67.4
85 & over	10,600	24,100	43.9
Total	1,800,200	1,825,900	98.6

The differences in the numbers of males and females were not uniform across age groups in both years. For the younger age groups (those aged less than 25) the male excess was more pronounced in 1996 than it was 50 years previously. For those aged 25-34 and 35-44 in 1996, emigration in the 1980s had the effect of reducing the number of males to a greater extent than the number of females. This distortion due to emigration was less pronounced in 1946.

The relatively greater gains in female life expectancy over the period, coupled with the higher level of male emigration in the 1950s, resulted in a marked deterioration of the sex ratio for those aged 65 and over.

AGE DISTRIBUTION

Population by single year of age

An indication of the change in the age structure of the population between 1946 and 1996 is provided by comparing the relevant populations classified by single year of age. The age structure at any point in time is affected by past demographic events such as births, deaths and migration flows. In particular, the fall in the number of births since 1980 is clearly indicated in the graph of the 1996 data.

Apart from the population aged 0-4 years, the numbers in each single year age group in 1996 exceeded the corresponding 1946 numbers. On average, the 1946 population was about 1½ years younger than the 1996 one.

IRISH TRADE JOURNAL
AND
STATISTICAL BULLETIN

IRISLEAbAR CRÁDÁLA AZUS FEASACÁN
SCAICISCIÐEAĊCA NA hÉIREANN

| VOL. XXIV. No. 1. | MARCH, 1949 | Price 4D. |

SINGLE PERSONS

Examining the population aged 15 years and over in 1946 and 1996, it is evident that a greater proportion of the relevant population was single (never having been married) in the earlier period. The greater propensity to remain single during the 1940s held for both males and females in urban and rural locations. The disparity was most pronounced for rural males aged 35-44. Just over half of this age group was single in 1946 compared with one in five some 50 years later.

Percentage single by age group

1946

Age	Urban		Rural	
	Males	Females	Males	Females
15-24	96.0	90.5	98.4	91.1
25-34	57.0	48.4	77.1	48.2
35-44	29.1	31.8	50.5	28.6
45-54	22.9	28.9	36.8	23.5
55-64	23.5	27.8	32.8	22.3
65 & over	23.7	28.7	26.0	20.7
15 & over	49.3	48.7	57.9	42.1

1996

Age	Urban		Rural	
	Males	Females	Males	Females
15-24	98.6	97.1	98.7	96.2
25-34	55.5	46.8	54.2	33.8
35-44	19.0	17.1	20.9	9.3
45-54	13.4	11.8	18.7	7.4
55-64	14.1	13.7	24.6	9.4
65 & over	17.0	21.0	29.0	14.7
15 & over	45.1	41.3	44.8	31.4

In general, rural males displayed a greater likelihood to remain single than their urban counterparts in 1946 (57.9% versus 49.3%). In fact, this relationship was prevalent for each age group at that time. However, by 1996 the urban and rural rates for males had equalised.

City-based females were more likely to remain single in 1946 and 1996 than women located in rural areas. By 1996 the urban/rural gap for females had widened considerably, especially for those aged 25-44 years.

Nearly 97% of the 1946 population were born in the Republic of Ireland. By 1996 this had fallen to 93%. The proportion of those born in Northern Ireland was identical in both periods (1.1%), while the influence exerted by the rest of the United Kingdom had grown greatly by 1996. Given the high outward migration to Britain during the 1950s and the latter half of the 1980s, the 1996 figure was probably affected to a significant extent by the immigration of children of returning Irish-born parents in the 1970s and 1990s.

Population by country of birth, 1946 and 1996

	1946		1996	
Country of birth	Number	%	Number	%
Ireland	2,856,200	96.7	3,344,900	93.0
Northern Ireland	33,500	1.1	39,600	1.1
Great Britain	49,400	1.7	151,100	4.2
Rest of the EU	1,800	0.1	19,200	0.5
Rest of Europe	1,200	0.0	3,600	0.1
USA	8,500	0.3	15,600	0.4
Rest of the World	4,400	0.1	22,500	0.6
Total	2,955,100	100.0	3,596,500	100.0

The influence of Ireland's accession to the EEC in 1973 is borne out by the increased share of persons born in the EU (as defined in 1996) in the overall total for 1996 compared with 1946. The number of US-born persons nearly doubled over the 50-year period, while the increase for the rest of the world was more than five-fold.

Within the State, an illustration of the increased mobility of the population in general is provided by analysing the percentage of the population enumerated in their county of birth. In the 1946 census, four out of five persons were enumerated in their county of birth, ranging from a low of 71.7% for Leinster to a high of 89.5% for Connacht. The overall percentage had fallen to 74% by 1996, and the provincial variability had greatly diminished (70.9% for Leinster to 78.8% for Ulster (part)).

HOUSEHOLDS AND LIVING CONDITIONS

Between 1946 and 1996 the number of private households increased from 662,654 to 1,114,974 (+68.3%). The number of one-person households more than trebled since 1946, while there was a doubling of the number of households containing two persons. Overall average household size has fallen from 4.2 in 1946 to 3.1 in 1996. Most of this decrease occurred in the most recent twenty-five year period as a direct result of declining fertility levels and increasing household formation.

Private households by size (000)

Number of persons	1946	1971	1996
1	69	103	238
2	119	149	255
3	116	116	179
4	103	102	191
5	84	84	133
6	63	65	70
7	44	44	32
8	29	27	10
9	18	16	4
10 & over	17	20	3
Total	663	726	1,115

It is also of interest to examine the housing characteristics of private households over the last half century. Information for 1946 is compared with that of 1991 — the last census year for which data on household characteristics are available. The composition of households, in terms of number of rooms, changed significantly as illustrated in the graph.

In 1946 less than a third of households had more than four rooms. By 1971 this had increased to 46.3%, and by 1991 the figure had reached

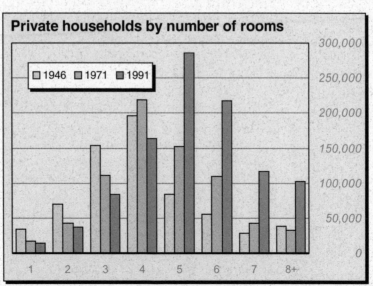

Private households by number of rooms

70.8%. The graph clearly shows that the number of small-sized households decreased steadily while those with five or more rooms grew rapidly.

Over 400,000 households in 1946 (61.3% of the total) did not have a piped water supply. However, nearly 230,000 of these used either a private well or private pump for their water supply. By 1991 the number of households reported as not having a piped water supply had diminished to 12,600.

Of the quarter of a million households that had piped water in 1946, just over 100,000 had the use of a fixed bath or shower. This represented 15% of all households at the time. The corresponding figure for 1991 was 94%.

Nearly a half of the 660,000 households in 1946 had no sanitary facilities. The number of houses with flush toilets grew from just over 255,000 in 1946 to over 970,000 in 1991 while the use of chemical or dry closets decreased from 86,700 to 7,700.

The housing market in 1991 was dominated to a far greater extent by owner-occupiers than it was in 1946. In the earlier period, owner occupation accounted for 52.6% of all houses. By 1991 this had risen to nearly 80%. Hand in hand with this increase in owner occupation went the demise of the rented sector, from 280,000 units in 1946 to 180,000 in 1991. Average monthly rental payments in 1946 were 36.8 shillings (equivalent to £1.84). The 1991 equivalent was £104.13, representing an increase of over 180% in real terms (adjusted by the all-items Consumer Price Index).

PROSPECTS FOR THE FUTURE

Comparing the 1946 and 1996 populations gives a useful insight into the structural changes that have taken place during the intervening 50-year period. However, it is also instructive to look to the future and examine the factors that will impact on the population in the early part of the new millennium. The projections used are those contained in *Population and Labour Force Projections 2001-2031*, published by the CSO in July 1999. The assumptions underlying these projections are as follows:

- **Fertility**: Three different sets of fertility rates were assumed: high (F1), medium (F2) and low (F3). F1 is considered somewhat on the high side, while F2 may be considered to be somewhat conservative in the light of developments elsewhere in Europe.

- **Mortality**: Only one mortality assumption was made. It assumed an increase in survivorship rates consistent with gains in life expectancy at birth from 73.0 and 78.7 years for males and females respectively in 1995-97 to 77.8 and 84.0 years in 2030-32.

- **Migration**: Two migration assumptions were used. In the first (M1), immigration was assumed to continue but diminish for the duration of the projection period. In the second (M2), immigration was assumed to give way to emigration by 2011.

Combining the various assumptions gives rise to six population outcomes in the period to 2031. Under the highest of these (M1F1), the population is projected to increase to 4.768 million, while under the lowest (M2F3) the population is projected to settle at 3.955 million. The historic population since 1946 along with the highest and lowest variants of the projections to 2031 is illustrated in the graph.

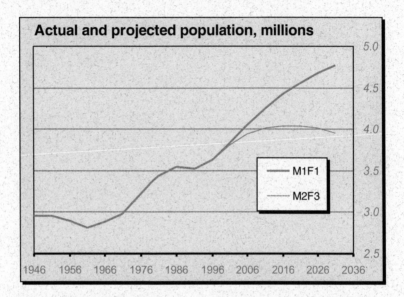

The most notable feature of the results is that the population is projected to increase in the period to 2031 under all combinations of assumptions. The main findings of the population projections in the period to 2031 can be summarised as follows:

- Under M2F3 the population aged 0-14 years is projected to fall to 569,000 by 2031, — a decrease of 46% compared with the 1981 peak of 1,044,000.

- Compared with 1996, the population is projected to contain fewer young persons and more old persons in 2031.

- The population aged 65 years and over is projected to double between 1996 and 2031, regardless of the combination of assumptions used.

- The very old population (those aged 80 and over) is projected to increase from its 1996 level of 90,000 to over 200,000 in 2031.

- The population of working age (15-64 years) will vary between 2.5 and 3 million persons, depending on the combination of assumption used, compared with a 1996 level of 2.4 million. Much of the increase will occur at the older end of the age distribution.

They ask for it!

ROWNTREE'S
MILK CHOCOLATE
2d DIVIDED BAR

and mother knows its food!

Made by
ROWNTREE & CO.
(Ireland) Ltd.
THE COCOA WORKS, DUBLIN

Matters of Life and Death

Mary Heanue

INTRODUCTION

Vital Statistics — statistics on births, deaths and marriages — are collected worldwide and are fundamental for comparing demographic and health characteristics of populations. For Ireland, the statistics are available since 1864. The CSO is responsible for their compilation from the civil registration systems for births, deaths and marriages, supplemented by returns from doctors, hospitals, coroners and the Gardai in the case of the classification of deaths by cause. This chapter deals with births and deaths; marriages are considered in Chapter 3.

BIRTHS AND FERTILITY

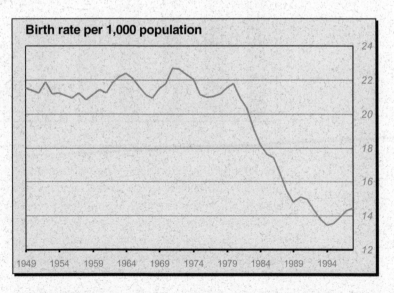

Birth rate per 1,000 population

Over the past 50 years, significant changes have occurred in Irish fertility. While the overall birth rate remained relatively stable until the early eighties, since then there has been a dramatic fall. The crude birth rate is the number of live births divided by the total population. This has fallen from 21.5 babies born per 1,000 persons in 1949 to 14.5 in 1998. The

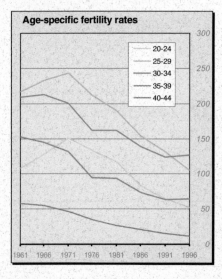

Age-specific fertility rates

Legend:
- 20-24
- 25-29
- 30-34
- 35-39
- 40-44

rate fell to its lowest point of 13.5 between 1994 and 1995 but since then there has been a small upturn.

The number of births is determined by the number of women in the fertile age groups and by their fertility levels. For a particular age group, the age-specific fertility rate is defined to be the number of births per 1,000 women in that age group. The graph shows how much Irish fertility rates have fallen in the past quarter century. For example, for women in the 25-29 age group, a quarter gave birth in 1971, whereas in 1998 only a tenth of such women gave birth.

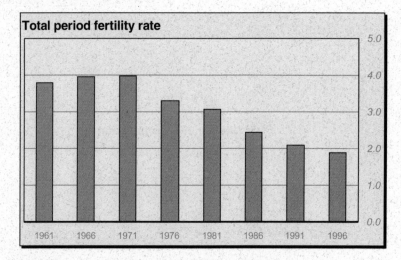

Total period fertility rate

The total period fertility rate is derived from the age-specific rates. It gives the theoretical average number of children who would be born alive to a woman during her lifetime if she were to pass through her childbearing years conforming to the age-specific fertility rates of a given period. This has fallen by more than a half in the past 30 years. It is generally considered that, in the absence of migration, population numbers can be maintained only if the total period fertility rate remains above 2.1. In Ireland, it dropped below this level in 1989, dropped below 2.0 three years later, and now stands at about 1.9. Despite the decline, we continue to have one of the highest rates in Western Europe.

Another striking change is that the proportion of births outside marriage has, as the graph shows, risen very sharply in the past 20 years, from 4% in 1978 to 28% in 1998. Indeed, it is now higher than the EU average. In

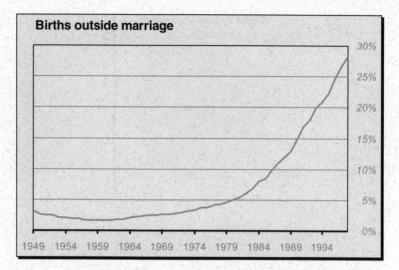

Births outside marriage

1996, 23% of all births in the EU occurred outside marriage and for Ireland the figure was 25%. The highest reported figure was from Sweden at 54% and the lowest was from Italy at 8%. This rise in births outside marriage may reflect changes in attitudes in Ireland today. A birth outside marriage does not necessarily mean a birth to a lone parent: many cohabiting couples now choose to have children outside the institution of marriage.

Births are not evenly distributed through the year: there is a seasonal effect, notably in the 4th quarter when fewest births occur. Seasonality in the 1940s was related to the seasonality of marriages; births started early in married life, and so the mid-year peak in births in 1949 corresponded to an autumn peak in marriages in the previous year. Seasonality in births remains in the 1990s and may be caused to some extent by planned pregnancies. Planning, albeit of a different type, is reflected in the smaller number of births on Saturdays and Sundays, an effect that has become more pronounced in recent years. While Saturday's child will work for its living and Sunday's child will never want, we find that significantly fewer children are born on these days than during the remainder of the week.

It is a biological fact that more boys are born than girls. The sex ratio is 1.05 boys for every girl. Over the years, the male excess in Ireland has varied from 4% to 8% and averaged 6%.

FEWER BIRTHS AND SMALLER FAMILIES

A high average age at maternity affects fertility because it lessens the time available to have children. Ireland's average age at maternity, always high by international standards, has been increasing in recent years. In the past, our large families compensated for this, but, now that our family size is dropping, our high average age at maternity is having its expected effect on births.

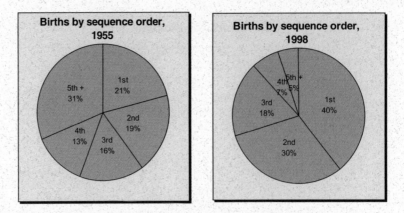

The overall drop in births is principally associated with the decrease in Irish family size. An interesting change that occurred, especially in the 1960s, is the increase in first time births or new families. The percentage of births accounted for by mothers with no previous children doubled to 40% over the past half-century.

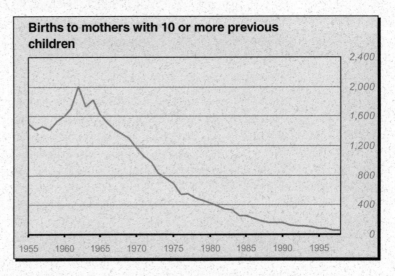

In 1962, there were over 2,000 births to mothers that had 10 or more previous children. There were only 55 such births in 1998.

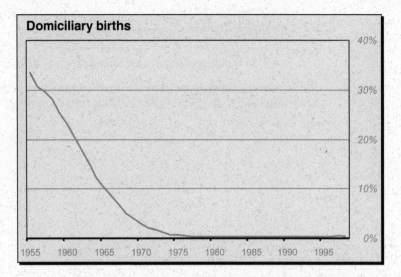

Another notable change over the years is the virtual disappearance of domiciliary (or home) births. Such births have dropped from one in three births in the early 1950s to only four in every thousand in 1998.

DEATHS

Mortality has improved steadily in Ireland over the past 50 years. The crude death rate — the number of deaths divided by the total population — has fallen from 12.7 per 1,000 persons in 1949 to 8.5 in 1998.

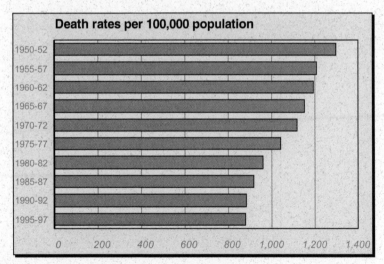

Mortality data provide useful information on how society is organised. While the rate of mortality is influenced by factors such as the age distribution of the population, there has nonetheless been a clear improvement in mortality over the years. Better medical services, housing, sanitation and nutrition all lead to better health and improved mortality.

The table gives the death rates per 100,000 corresponding population by age group. There has been a huge drop in the death rates, especially for the younger age groups. This can be explained by the dramatic drop in infant mortality and infectious diseases such as tuberculosis.

Death rates per 100,000 corresponding population

Age group	Rate 1949		Rate 1998	
	Males	Females	Males	Females
0-4	1,511	1,259	177	132
5-9	95	89	10	11
10-14	73	91	22	19
15-19	153	138	84	31
20-24	230	247	139	31
25-34	263	327	120	39
35-44	426	423	168	98
45-54	940	723	397	255
55-64	1,977	1,610	1,255	722
65-74	4,657	4,174	3,701	2,078
75 & over	13,388	12,319	11,806	8,840

Indeed, the improvement in infant mortality has been the main contributor to this overall drop in mortality. Infant mortality is seen as an indicator of the health and social conditions in a country. Moreover, the drop in maternal deaths from about 100 a year in 1949 to an average of less than one a year nowadays also reflects the improved health and obstetric services, female education, access to hospitals and blood transfusions, as well as an improved social and economic environment. Although present-day infant mortality in Ireland at 6 per 1,000 live births compares well with that of our European neighbours, it is still almost double that of the Nordic countries.

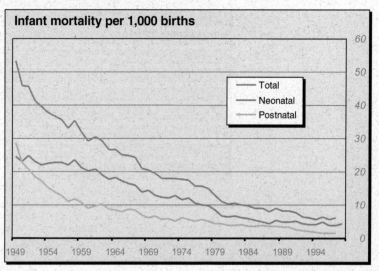

Infant mortality per 1,000 births

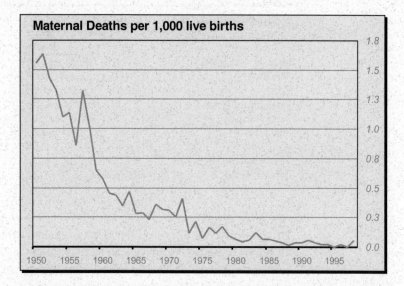

Maternal Deaths per 1,000 live births

In 1949, 65% of deaths occurred at home, while only 22% occurred there in 1998. This shows the greater availability and utilisation of institutional care. Such care is no longer confined to hospitals but now includes a wide variety of community care establishments such as nursing homes, welfare homes, hospices and sheltered accommodation.

In 1949, 11% of deaths were uncertified while today only 0.05% are uncertified. The percentage of coroner inquests and postmortems rose from 3% to 13% in the same period.

CAUSES OF DEATH

The underlying causes of death in Ireland is currently coded in accordance with the 9th Revision of the *International Statistical Classification of Diseases, Injuries and Causes of Death*. Now a 10th revision is available, reflecting developments in medical knowledge. With ten fundamental revisions over the past century, it is hard to make comparisons. Each revision has different underlying rules which effect the causes of death assigned. For example, prior to the 7th revision, a heart attack was not distinguished in the classification and therefore did not exist statistically as a cause of death. Also, senility is now rarely given as an underlying cause of death on a medical death certificate.

The table gives a percentage breakdown of the principal causes of deaths reported in 1949 and 1998.

Causes of death

1949		1998	
Heart disease	26.3%	Heart disease	23.0%
Senility	14.7%	Cancer	23.9%
Cancer	10.9%	Cerebrovascular	8.2%
Intracranial lesions	7.5%	Pneumonia	7.2%
Tuberculosis	7.1%	Injury and poisoning	4.9%
Pneumonia	3.5%	Other causes	32.8%
Bronchitis	2.7%		
Injury and poisoning	2.6%		
Other causes	24.7%		
Total	100.0%	Total	100.0%

To compare the two lists properly, one needs to look at the ages at which the deaths occurred. Pneumonia, on face value, has doubled from 1,329 deaths in 1949 to 2,244 deaths in 1998. On further examination, however, we see that 85% of these deaths in 1998 occurred at ages 75 and over, whereas in 1949, 44% of pneumonia deaths occurred to those aged under 5. In 1998, half of the injury and poisoning deaths occurred in the 15-44 age group. These were mainly due to suicide and road traffic accidents. There is no such trend in the 1949 data as the mortality was evenly spread across all ages.

Deaths from infectious diseases such as tuberculosis and influenza, very common in the early part of the century, are now much rarer. This is mainly due to specific vaccinations against certain diseases. From the

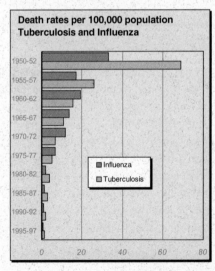

beginning to the end of this century, there has been a transition worldwide in causes of death, from infectious to non-infectious and chronic diseases, such as heart disease and cancer.

In the past, tuberculosis in particular affected huge numbers of young adults: half of all deaths of people aged 25-34 in 1949 were from tuberculosis. In the same year it accounted for a mortality of 91 per 100,000 population compared to one per 100,000 population in 1998. Similarly, the incidence of the disease has fallen from 230 new cases per 100,000 population in 1952 to 12 per 100,000 population in 1998. One of the results of this has been the shutdown throughout the country of the many sanatoria that had once been a feature of Irish life. The disease has not however been completely eradicated.

While deaths from diseases such as smallpox and diphtheria have become a thing of the past, new diseases have arrived. The most prominent of these is probably AIDS, which appeared in the 1980s. Deaths from AIDS in Ireland peaked in the first half of the 1990s, with over 40 deaths each year from 1992 to 1995, but the numbers of deaths have fallen significantly since then.

The table gives a percentage breakdown of the principal causes of death in 1949 and 1998 for children aged 1 to 4. While allowing for the fluctuations in the low incidence, it is clear that the principal causes of death have changed significantly over the 50-year period in question.

Deaths of children aged 1-4

1949		1998	
Pneumonia	18.1%	Injury and poisoning	26.6%
Tuberculosis	14.8%	Congenital anomalies	23.4%
Diarrhoea, enteritis	6.6%	Sudden infant death	12.0%
Congenital anomalies	5.1%	Cancer	9.3%
Whooping cough	4.7%	Pneumonia	7.8%
Measles	3.3%	Leukaemia	3.1%
Bronchitis	2.6%		
Diphtheria	1.0%		
Total number	723	Total number	64

The change in the level of infectious diseases in children is very clear. In the past, the early years of a child's life — particularly the first year — amounted to a significant hurdle; in 1949, one child in 16 did not live to see his or her fifth birthday, whereas in 1998 the ratio was one in 136. In 1949, 13.4% of infants (children under the age of one) died of diarrhoea and enteritis, 13.3% of pneumonia, 2.7% of whooping cough and 1.9% of bronchitis.

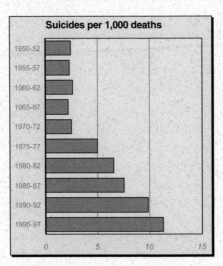

While allowing for the fact that there was an understatement of suicide in the past, there is however a definite trend upwards in the suicide rates in recent times, particularly among males aged 15-24. This trend is also true internationally.

A special effort is made by the CSO to improve the accuracy of suicide statistics with the help of a confidential statistical returns completed by the Gardai since 1967.

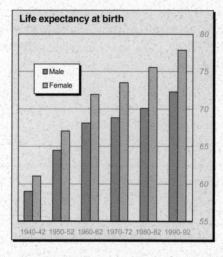

Life expectancy at birth

Male
Female

1940-42 1950-52 1960-62 1970-72 1980-82 1990-92

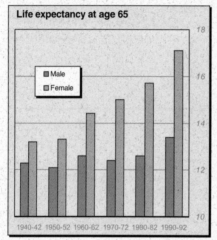

Life expectancy at age 65

Male
Female

1940-42 1950-52 1960-62 1970-72 1980-82 1990-92

In Ireland, as in other countries, there is a marked difference between male and female life expectancies: women live on average 5½ years longer than men. The life expectancy for males in Ireland is now 72.3 years, and 77.9 years for females.

As mortality rates have decreased, life expectancy has increased. Between the early 1940s and early 1990s, Irish male life expectancy increased by 13 years or 23%, while for females the increase was 17 years or 28%. On examining similar trends for 65 year old males, we see that their life expectancy has increased by little more than one year or 9% while for women the increase is much more significant at 4 years or 30%.

The graph below compares life expectancy in 1960 and 1990 in a number of European countries. While life expectancy in Ireland has increased, it is generally lower than in the other countries, and the improvement over the years has been less marked. Ranking life expectancy among the 13 countries in the table, Ireland was ranked 5th in 1960 for males but now has dropped to 11th place. For females, Ireland has remained at 12th place.

For people aged 65, the life expectancy is lower than for the other countries. For men aged 65, the expectancy in 1990 was 13.3 years, while for the other 12 countries here it ranged from 14.0 to 15.7 years. For women aged 65, expectancy was 16.9 years compared to 17-20 years for the other countries.

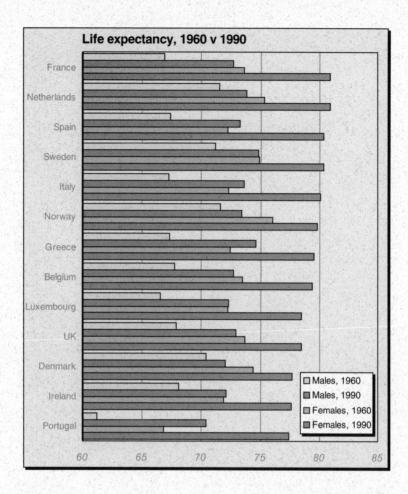

Life expectancy, 1960 v 1990

Countries (top to bottom): France, Netherlands, Spain, Sweden, Italy, Norway, Greece, Belgium, Luxembourg, UK, Denmark, Ireland, Portugal

Legend:
- ☐ Males, 1960
- ■ Males, 1990
- ▨ Females, 1960
- ▨ Females, 1990

Axis: 60 65 70 75 80 85

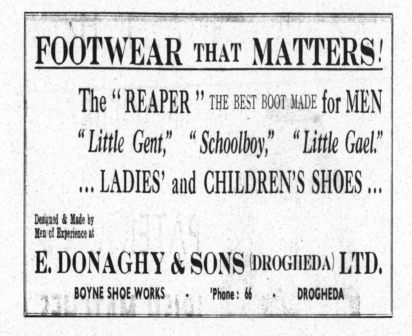

HOT BATHS for the WHOLE FAMILY

from the same fire that cooks their meals

THE "AB" cooker
COMBINING COOKING & WATER HEATING IN ONE UNIT

WITH an "A.B." Cooker in your kitchen the fuel you use for cooking also gives you a constant service of piping

Aspects of Society

Adrian Redmond, Mary Heanue

3

EDUCATION

Basic education in the 1940s was provided to the mass of the population by a system of church-controlled state-supported National schools, the vast majority of which were one- or two-teacher schools. Secondary schools (also largely controlled by the churches) provided further fee-paying education for a privileged minority, while the state-supported Vocational sector provided a largely technical education. Many pupils did not complete their primary education, few went on to second level, and only a tiny proportion reached third level. According to the Census of Population, 35,000 children aged 15 or under were gainfully occupied in 1946, half of these in the agricultural sector.

There have been many changes since 1950. Enrolment in Secondary schools increased, particularly from the late 1960s onwards. This was caused by economic growth, the Free Education Scheme of 1967, the raising of the school-leaving age to 15 in 1972, and the rising population. Corporal punishment was abolished. Many new subjects were introduced. New types of school — Comprehensive and Community schools — were started. In the late 1960s and the 1970s, the National Institutes of Higher Education and the Regional Technical Colleges were established, resulting in a big expansion in the number of third-level full-time students in the technological sector.

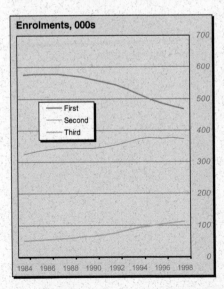

Enrolments, 000s
First
Second
Third

In 1998, a grand total of 952,000 students of all ages were in full-time education. More than half of the students at first level were male — more boys are born than girls — but significantly more than half of those at second and third level were female. While the total has changed little since the early 1980s, the distribution between levels has altered, as the graph shows: the numbers at primary level have been falling since 1985 (driven by the fall in the birth rate), and the numbers at third level have been rising.

The table, giving Census of Population figures for the numbers of fulltime students aged 15 and over, shows the growth in the quarter century since 1971.

Fulltime students

	1971	1981	1991	1996
15-19	121,000	177,300	239,000	264,800
20-24	13,800	19,900	39,000	62,400
25-29	1,600	2,100	3,200	6,700
30 and over	400	1,100	1,900	5,700
Total	136,900	200,300	283,100	339,600

By 1998, there were 3,350 first level schools and 800 second level institutions (including Secondary, Vocational, Community and Comprehensive schools). The number of third level institutions had increased to 59. This included 7 universities, 7 teacher training colleges, 13 institutes of technology, 10 religious institutions, and 17 other non-aided institutions. There were also 132,000 people enrolled in Adult Education courses in Vocational, Community or Comprehensive Schools in 1998, of which 73% were female.

PRIMARY EDUCATION

As a result of the School Attendance Act, 1926 (which applied to children between their 6th and their 14th birthdays), the number of pupils in National schools rose sharply to a high of 522,000 in 1926, a record that was not to be beaten until 1975. From the mid-1960s to the mid-1980s,

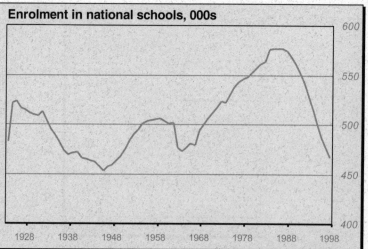

Enrolment in national schools, 000s

the numbers rose, driven largely by the trend in the population aged 4 to 12 years old, and reached an all-time high of 577,000 in 1985. In the 13 years since then, however, enrolment fell very sharply by 110,000 to 467,000.

In 1950, the Primary School Certificate Examination was the first hurdle faced by students. It covered Irish, English and arithmetic, and was compulsory for all pupils in sixth class. The certificate was accepted by employers as evidence of the standard of education of applicants for employment or apprenticeship. The examination was abolished in 1967.

National schools

	Schools	Teachers	Pupils
1950	4,890	12,900	464,000
1998	3,300	21,100	461,000

There were 4,890 National schools in 1950. While there were plenty of large schools — there were 131 with a daily attendance of over 400 — most were very small. Over a thousand schools had a daily attendance of less than 30. The pupil/teacher ratio was about 34 through the 1950s and 1960s, but this masked huge differences. While the average class size in one-teacher schools was 15, many pupils in urban areas were in classes of more than 50. This variability was reduced through a policy of amalgamating the smaller schools. In 1970, about a third of pupils were in classes of size 45 or over, and by 1998, there were only 17 classes of over 40 pupils, containing 752 pupils. In 1972, the number of National schools fell below 4,000 and now there are about 3,300 National schools. In 1998, the average class size was 26, and the average number of teachers per school was 6.

In 1950, there were 4,200 male and 8,700 female teachers. By 1998, the number of male teachers had changed little, but the number of female teachers had doubled. The proportion of lay teachers has also increased: in 1970, nearly one in five teachers were members of religious orders, mainly nuns; by 1998, this had fallen to only 3%.

In 1950, over 500 schools were all-Irish, 51 in Dublin. By 1998, the number of all-Irish schools had fallen to 223, covering 6% of all pupils.

SECONDARY EDUCATION

The table (from the Department of Education's Report, 1949-50) shows the changes in the numbers of Secondary schools and pupils over the quarter of a century to 1950. The number of schools increased from 284 to 416 and the number of pupils more than doubled to 47,000. Despite this increase, only a small proportion of children made the transition from primary to secondary education. The table also shows that more

Tá líon na Meán-Scol maille le líon a gcuid scoláirí ag dul i méid i gcónaí. Cífear ó na figiúirí seo leanas an borradh adhbal-mór atá tagt́a iontu san aram̆ le 25 bliana anall : —

Scoil-ḃliaɴ, 1924-'25						buaċailli	Cailíɴi
Líon na Scol do ḃuaċailli	135	Líon na Scoláirí	...			13,671	—
Líon na Scol do ċailíni	122	,,	,,	,,	...	—	8,346
Líon na Scol don dá ċineál	27	,,	,,	,,	...	553	461
		Iomlán na Scoláirí			=	14,224	8,807
Iomlán na Scol	= 284				=	23,031	
Scoil-ḃliaɴ, 1949-'50						buaċailli	Cailíɴi
Líon na Scol do ḃuaċailli	183	Líon na Scoláirí	...			24,130	—
Líon na Scol do ċailíni	188	,,	,,	,,		—	20,319
Líon na Scol don dá ċineál	45	,,	,,	,,	...	1,312	1,304
		Iomlán na Scoláirí			=	25,442	21,623
Iomláɴ na Scol	= 416				=	47,065	

boys than girls availed of secondary education, though this gap narrowed a lot between 1925 and 1950.

In 1950, the dropout rate was high: there were 10,200 Intermediate Certificate candidates but only 4,500 Leaving Certificate candidates. Two decades later, in 1970, the number of Intermediate candidates had increased to 35,900 and the number of Leaving candidates to 19,000. By 1998, about 80% of those entering secondary schools reached the final examination: there were 65,600 Junior Certificate (which had replaced the Intermediate Certificate) and 61,000 Leaving Certificate school candidates.

In contrast to the Secondary schools, which were essentially private institutions, the Vocational schools owed their existence to State action. In 1950, the number of students in Vocational schools was 86,000. This

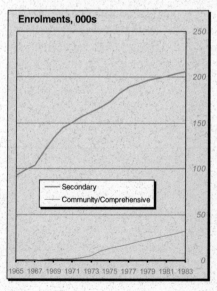

Enrolments, 000s

Secondary

Community/Comprehensive

250
200
150
100
50
0

1965 1967 1969 1971 1973 1975 1977 1979 1981 1983

was greater than the number in Secondary Schools, but 80% of those in the Vocational Schools were part-timers. More than two-thirds were over 16.

Comprehensive schools had arrived during the 1960s, and by 1970 there were four such schools, with a total of 1,473 pupils. In 1998, of the 368,000 full-time pupils in second level schools, 59% were in Secondary schools, 26% in Vocational schools, and the remainder in Community or Comprehensive schools. The big increase in the numbers at second level took place between the mid-1960s and the early 1980s. During this period, the enrolment in Secondary schools more than doubled, and the enrolment in the new Community and Comprehensive schools rose to 32,000. During the same period, the enrolment of fulltime second level students in Vocational schools also more than doubled to reach 75,000.

School sizes have been increasing. In 1950, only 16 of the 416 Secondary schools had over 300 pupils. The largest boys' school was O'Connell School (823 pupils) in North Richmond St, Dublin, and the largest girls' school was Coláiste San Dominic (443 pupils) in Eccles St, Dublin. In 1998, 357 of the 435 Secondary schools had over 300 pupils, and 35 had an enrolment of over 800. Two-thirds of second-level pupils are now in schools of over 500.

The number of teachers in secondary schools rose from 3,800 in 1950 to 12,700 in 1998. The numbers of second level teachers in religious orders were very high, but have fallen very sharply over the years: there were 3,700 in 1970, but only 740 in 1998.

The graphs show the numbers of boys and girls sitting the main Leaving Certificate subjects in 1950 and 1998. Apart from Irish, English and Mathematics, most students also took Geography, History and Latin in 1950. Technical Drawing was also very popular among both boys and girls. Girls accounted for all Domestic Science and Physiology & Hygiene candidates, and for the vast majority of candidates of French, while boys accounted for almost all candidates of Chemistry, Physics and Greek.

The main change in 1998 was the diversity of the subjects available, notably the rise of Biology, Business Organisation, German, Art, and Construction Studies, balanced somewhat by the virtual disappearance of Latin and Greek. There were significantly more girls taking French, Biology and Home Economics, and significantly more boys taking Geography, History, and especially Physics, Engineering, Construction Studies, and Technical Drawing. The range of languages available had greatly expanded by 1998, the most notable addition being Arabic with over 100 candidates.

There were 107 All-Irish Secondary schools in 1950; these contained 11,600 pupils. In 1998, there were 34 All-Irish second-level schools, containing 7,400 pupils.

THIRD LEVEL EDUCATION

In 1950, the number of fulltime students at the universities was only 7,900, of which only a quarter were female. Since then, there has been a big increase, especially since 1970. The number of fulltime students at

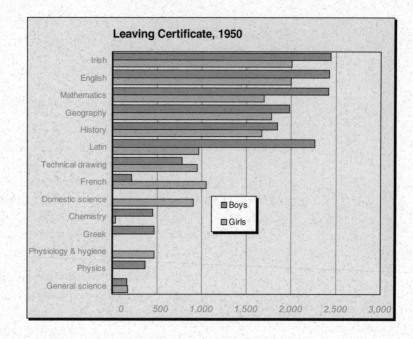

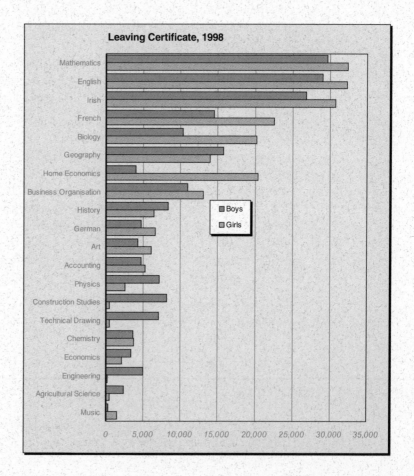

third level in 1970 was about 25,000, of which 18,600 were university students. By 1998, the number of students had more than quadrupled to 112,200, of which 61,300 were university students and 41,900 were students at the various Technological Colleges. The gender balance has also changed: the majority of students at third level are now female; in particular, 56% of university students in 1998 were female.

Only 1,100 undergraduate degrees were awarded in 1950; the annual number awarded is now more than 14 times greater. The increase in the number of postgraduate degrees is far more dramatic: there were only 116 such degrees awarded in 1950, but currently about 7,600 postgraduate degrees are awarded annually.

Census of Population results show that, in 1971, a total of 22,000 people had scientific or technological qualifications. By 1996, it had increased to 158,000.

REFORMATORY SCHOOLS AND INDUSTRIAL SCHOOLS

In 1950, there were 3 Reformatories and 51 Industrial Schools in the country, all run by religious orders. Children were committed to these schools by the Metropolitan Children's Court or the various District Courts. In July 1950, there were 210 offenders (172 boys and 38 girls) under detention in the three Reformatories in the country. They were between 13 and 17 years of age. The boys were held in the large Reformatory School at Daingean, County Offaly, and the girls were divided between Limerick and Kilmacud in Dublin. The number of committals during that school year was 97, the usual grounds being theft, housebreaking or similar offences.

The 51 Industrial Schools were widely dispersed around Ireland, and varied a lot in size. The largest Industrial School for boys was in Artane, Dublin (776 children were detained there in July 1950). The largest Industrial School for girls was Goldenbridge, Dublin (148).

One of the most extraordinary social differences between the 1940s and now relates to the extent to which children were committed to Industrial Schools. In 1950, 6,000 children were under detention in such schools. It is perhaps surprising that slightly more than half of these children were girls. During the year, the number of committals was 833, the number discharged was 994, and 31 children absconded. Of the 833 children committed, over two-thirds were less than 10 years old, and most of the rest were under 14. Half were on the grounds of not having a settled place of abode or visible means of subsistence or having parents or guardians who did not exercise proper guardianship, 23% on the grounds of destitution, 8% for begging, 7% for not complying with a School Attendance Order, 4% because they were "uncontrollable", and most of the rest because they were charged with an offence punishable, in the case of an adult, with penal servitude.

By 1960, the number under detention in Industrial Schools fell below 4,000, and it fell to 1,270 in 1970. Artane, which had a capacity of 830, had only 10 boys that year. The following year, the Reformatory and Industrial Schools were reclassified as Special Schools and Residential Homes. There were 6 Special Schools and 27 Residential Homes. By 1998, the number of institutions — Special Schools for Young Offenders — was only six. The total number of children in detention was 127, of which 11 were girls. The number of full-time staff was 302.

IRISH SPEAKERS

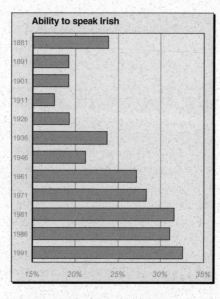

Ability to speak Irish

1881
1891
1901
1911
1926
1936
1946
1961
1971
1981
1986
1991

15%   20%   25%   30%   35%

The Census of Population included a question on the ability to speak the Irish language. While difficult to measure because of the effects of personal judgement, the comparison across time has some validity. As the graph shows, there was a big fall between 1881 and 1891. It fell to a low of less than 18% in 1911, but then started to climb. By 1936, the decline was reversed and in recent censuses the percentage has been over 30%.

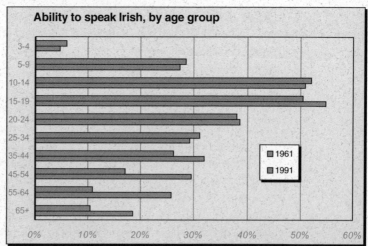

Ability to speak Irish, by age group

3-4
5-9
10-14
15-19
20-24
25-34
35-44
45-54
55-64
65+

☐ 1961
☐ 1991

0%   10%   20%   30%   40%   50%   60%

Part of increase was caused by the changing population structure. The percentage who can speak Irish varies a lot for different age groups, and it is highest for those aged 10-19. There are higher numbers of people now in those age groups. Moreover, children remain in the educational system much longer than in the past. But this cannot explain all the difference, because there has also been increases for other age groups. Comparing the age distribution of speakers in 1961 and 1991 shows that there were big increases for those aged 35 and over.

The question asked in the 1996 Census was not comparable with that used in previous censuses. In 1996, the concentration was on the actual speaking of the language as opposed to the ability to speak it. The results show that a total of 354,000 people spoke Irish daily (80% of these were aged 19 or under), 124,000 spoke it weekly, and 525,000 spoke it less often.

MARRIAGES

Marriage, in recent years, has become less popular.

There were 16,000 marriages in 1949, and 15,600 in 1997. This modest fall masks a considerable change in the marriage rate, because, while the number of marriages has changed little, the population has increased so that the marriage rate has, as the graph shows, fallen considerably. The marriage rate stayed very steady for a few years after 1949, but then rose steeply in the late 1960s and early 1970s. After peaking in 1973 (7.4 per 1,000 population), the rate had declined fairly steadily for the last quarter century and it is now lower than ever before — about 4.5 per 1,000.

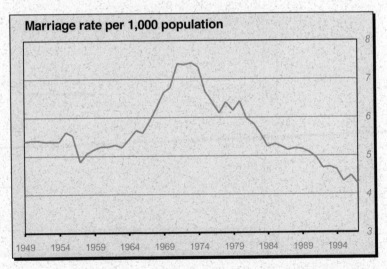

Marriage rate per 1,000 population

In tandem with the fall in the number of marriages, there has been an increasing proportion of civil marriages. Until the 1970s, these accounted for less than 1% of all marriages. This passed 3% in the mid-1980s, and reached almost 6% in 1995. (The sudden peak in 1983 arose from a tax concession for couples who married before the end of the tax year.)

In 1946, a high proportion of people was single. There were no doubt many reasons for this. One factor was the remarkable geographic varia-

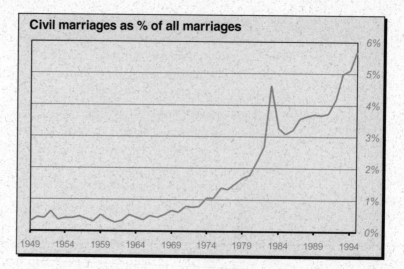

Civil marriages as % of all marriages

tion in the distribution of the sexes. There were more women than men only in the cities. The ratio was lowest in Dun Laoghaire, where there were only 730 males per 1,000 females. The ratio for Dublin city was 839. Elsewhere there were more men than women, notably in Cavan, Leitrim, and especially in Offaly where there were 1,200 men per 1,000 women. In 1996, the variation was far less. The ratios for Dublin and the cities were lower than for the other counties, though Galway City was the only place where it dropped below 900. The highest ratio of men per women was in Leitrim (1,086).

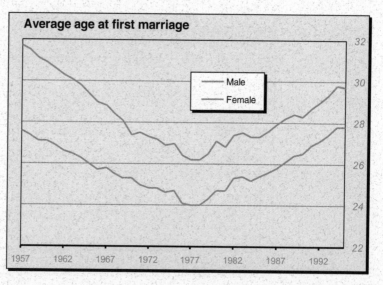

Average age at first marriage

Since 1946, the proportion of people remaining single has fallen. For example, for the 50-54 age group, 28% were single in 1946, but only 13% of this age group were single in 1996.

The graph shows the average age at first marriage from 1957. There was a fall in the average age until the late 1970s, but since then it has risen. The graph also shows that the average age is always higher for men than for women but that this gap has narrowed from 4 years to 2 years.

As the marriage rate declined, there has been an increase in family units not based on traditional marriage. The table shows that, of 807,000 family units in Ireland in 1996, 32,000 consisted of cohabiting couples, with or without children. An even bigger component is the number of family units based on a lone parent.

Family units, 1996

	Family units	Children
Husband and wife without children	155,000	–
Husband and wife with children	492,000	1,206,000
Cohabiting couple without children	19,000	–
Cohabiting couple with children	13,000	23,000
Lone mother with children	108,000	203,000
Lone father with children	21,000	38,000
Total family units	807,000	1,470,000

Ireland is experiencing increasing levels of marital instability. In the 1991 census, 55,100 persons were enumerated with a marital status of separated or divorced. This figure had risen by 60% to 87,800 in the 1996 census.

RELIGION

There was a consistent decline in the numbers of non-Roman Catholics since the middle of the 19th century, especially in the period 1911-1926 when the numbers fell from 327,000 to 221,000. While migration contributed to the decline, it also arose because the Roman Catholic birth rate was relatively high and their death rate was relatively low. The followers of the "traditional" religions — Church of Ireland (this category includes Protestants), Presbyterians, Methodist, Jews — were significantly older that the rest of the population.

The religions were more geographically concentrated in the past. For example, in 1946 less than half the population of the town of Greystones was Roman Catholic, but by 1991 this had risen to four-fifths. In 1946, non-Roman Catholics tended to be relatively highly represented in certain occupations, notably employers, managers, large farmers, chemical workers, clerks, bank officials, etc, but now they are much more evenly distributed.

In 1891, 89% of the population was Roman Catholic. This rose to 94% in 1946 and fell back to 92% in 1991. (The last census in which Religion was asked was 1991.) The graph shows the changing distribution of non-Roman Catholic religions in the century from 1891 to 1991. There were many changes in the size and distribution of the "Other" category, particularly in the decade between 1981 and 1991. First, the number of people who left their religion unstated almost doubled to 83,000. Sec-

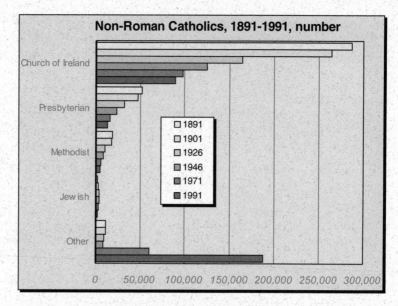

Non-Roman Catholics, 1891-1991, number

Church of Ireland

Presbyterian

Methodist

Jewish

Other

Legend:
- 1891
- 1901
- 1926
- 1946
- 1971
- 1991

0   50,000   100,000   150,000   200,000   250,000   300,000

ond, the number classified under "No Religion" increased massively from 8,000 to 66,000. And third, people with other stated religions increased from 6,000 to 39,000. Apart from 16,000 who gave their religion simply as Christian, this included 3,875 Muslims, 3,393 Jehovah's Witnesses, 986 Buddhists, 953 Hindus, 853 Latter Day Saints, 430 Baha'I, 358 Greek Orthodox, 202 Pantheists, and many other religions.

The Census results also show the decline in the numbers of clergy. In 1946, 18,300 people classified their occupation as Clergy. This fell to 6,500 in the 1996 Census. The distribution by age in 1996 clearly shows the effect of falling vocations: half of the clergy were aged 55 or over. While the fall in the number of male clergy was relatively modest (from 6,100 to 4,700), the fall for females — predominantly nuns — was very severe (from 12,100 to 1,900). As a proportion, females accounted for two-thirds of the clergy in 1946, but less than a third in 1996.

RADIO AND TELEVISION

Regular radio broadcasting began in Dublin on New Year's Day, 1926. The service was referred to by its call-sign of 2RN. Broadcasting from Cork began the following year, and reception became much more widespread when the Athlone transmitter came into service in 1933. The service became known as Radio Éireann in 1937.In 1949, the year the CSO was founded, about three-quarters of the population had coverage.

From 1926, licences for radio sets became compulsory. The graph shows the numbers of licences each year. The take-up was rapid during the 1930s. Towards the end of the war, the number of listeners fell, because, especially in rural areas, batteries were hard to get. The sharp rise resumed in 1948, and continued until 1961 when they reached a peak of a half a million. The numbers then fell off very sharply because, from

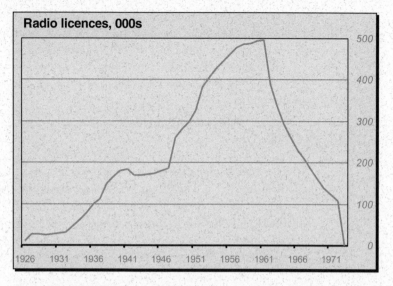

Radio licences, 000s

1962, television licences covered radio as well. Radio licences were abolished in 1972.

In 1949, there was only 7 hours of broadcasting a day: the afternoon slot was at 1-2:30pm and the evening one at 5:30-11pm. In 1952, a morning slot of an hour or so was added. Nowadays, of course, there are several national radio stations broadcasting in FM stereo around the clock, along with many commercial, local and community stations.

By the end of the 1970s, it is estimated that 95% of households and nearly half of cars had radios.

The CSO conducted a series of full-scale national listenership surveys for Radio Éireann during 1953-1955. These showed very high levels of listenership for the morning and evening slots, and extraordinarily high levels for the afternoon slots: in households with a radio, two-thirds tuned into the news at 1:30pm.

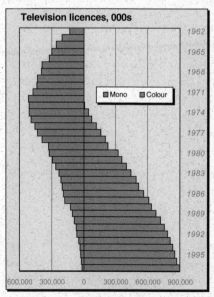

Television licences, 000s

Television was seen in Ireland for the first time in 1951 at a stand on the Spring Show at the RDS. During the 1950s, the East coast and border counties came within range of the expanding BBC television service. By 1958, it is estimated that there were 20,000 television sets in the country.

Telefís Éireann started transmission on the snowy New Year's Eve of 1961. Television ownership grew rapidly.

By 1966, over half of the homes in Ireland had a set. The total number of licences passed half a million in 1972. In 1973, a special licence for colour TVs was introduced. By 1980, colour licences accounted for half of all licences. The number of monochrome licences continued to fall steadily. In 1986, only 2% of licences were monochrome.

COMMUNICATIONS

The total number of items delivered by letter post in 1949 was 178 million. In 1997 it was nearly four times greater. The increase in recent years in the use of the telephone, and in electronic communications generally, does not seem to have had an effect on our use of the postal service, because the number of items delivered has continued to increase during the 1990s. Between 1996 and 1997 alone, the total increased by 69 million or 12%.

The first telephone exchange in Ireland was opened in Dublin in 1880. It was located in Commercial Buildings in Dame Street and it had five subscribers. In 1900, the Dublin exchange was moved to Crown Alley and its capacity was increased to 1,600 lines. By the end of the war in 1918 there were 12,500 subscribers' lines, of which half were in Dublin.

The service continued to expand, though still by 1949 very few households were privileged to possess a telephone: there were 43,000 exchange lines in the country, and only a third of these were residential. Many of the lines were manual, requiring operator intervention even for a local call. The total number of calls made was 68 million, corresponding to 1,581 calls per line. This amounted to only 23 calls per capita each year, or a call on average of once a fortnight. The cost of a three-minute call varied from ½p for a local call to 16p, the maximum within the State.

In 1997, the figures were very different. There were 1,427,000 exchange lines, and the total number of calls made was nearly eight billion (an increase of 30% on the previous year). The number of calls per capita in 1996 was about 2,100, so that on average each man, woman and child in the country made (and received) nearly six calls a day. The increase in telephone usage in the 1990s was higher than implied here because calls made from mobile phones are excluded.

CRIME AND PUNISHMENT

In 1949, Ireland was a peaceful country.

In County Laois on 29 May 1949, a young unmarried farmer died under suspicious circumstances at his home. A postmortem examination showed that he died from strychnine poisoning. His sister was charged, and at the Central Criminal Court on 21 November 1949 she was convicted of murder and sentenced to death. This was subsequently commuted to life imprisonment.

What makes this sad tale unusual — indeed unique — was that it was the only murder in the country in 1949. (It must be said, however, that there were also five cases of infanticide, which, in 1949, was a legal category separate from murder.)

In 1949, the modern methods of the day were used in crime detection: fingerprinting, microphotography, ballistics testing, and radio-controlled cars. Now, the Garda operate on horseback (Garda Mounted Unit), in the water (Garda Underwater Unit), in the sky (Garda Air Support Unit), and even internationally (on UN Peacekeeping Missions). Increasingly, they operate electronically; for example, a closed circuit TV surveillance system operates in the centre of Dublin. Another initiative in the war against crime was the popular weekly RTE programme, *Gárda Patrol*. This programme ceased some years ago, but the RTE *Crimeline* programme took up the baton in 1992. More recently, the Garda Bureau of Fraud Investigation was set up in 1995 to deal with complex serious cases of commercial fraud, including computer fraud and money laundering.

Organised violent crime existed in the 1940s, though it bore no relation to the organised crime of the 1990s. As the 1949 Garda Report succinctly states, "*17 organised crimes of violence were recorded on 1948, all of which were agrarian.*"

In the period from 1949 on, there was only one judicial execution: on 20 April 1954, a 24-year old man was hanged in Mountjoy. The death penalty was abolished in 1990.

In the statistics below, a distinction is drawn between non-indictable (or summary) offences and indictable offences. Non-indictable offences, such as failure to wear a seat-belt, may be processed to a conclusion by a District Court. Indictable offences, such as murder or armed robbery, may be tried by a judge and jury in higher courts. The figures for indictable offences relate to offences known or reported, while for non-indictable offences the figures relate to proceedings taken. The term "crime rate" is based on indictable offences. The distinction between the two categories of offence is not entirely satisfactory: some offences treated as indictable are not very serious, and some serious offences are treated as non-indictable.

Caution is required in looking at trends in crimes and offences over time, particularly when talking about the total number of indictable or non-indictable offences. There can be changes in the recording rules or in the level of reporting by the public. There were also many changes in the definition of offences, particularly summary offences; these relate to matters such as bye-laws, parking regulations, and the wearing of a seat belt.

Crime levels remained fairly steady through to the mid-1960s. After that, there was a change in the pattern of crime and levels rose. No doubt this was linked to the fact that Ireland was entering a period of rapid social and economic change. There were changes in industrialisation, urbanisation, migration, prosperity, car ownership, etc. From the mid-1960s, there were huge increases in, for example, housebreaking, robbery and indictable assaults.

Indictable offences

	1949	1998
Against the person		
Murder	1	38
Infanticide	5	–
Manslaughter, excluding traffic fatalities	9	13
Manslaughter: traffic fatalities	4	3
Assault and wounding	167	691
Other (mainly sexual)	310	1,162
Against property with violence		
Armed robbery	2	61
Arson	63	281
Malicious damage	277	8,223
Other (mainly burglary or robbery)	2,065	28,626
Larceny		
Larceny from person (pickpocket)	254	3,202
Larceny of motor vehicles	16	1,500
Larceny of pedal cycles	1,420	292
Larceny from unattended vehicles	944	12,377
Larceny from shops or stalls	923	7,688
Other larceny, fraud, embezzlement	5,573	21,068
Other		
Misuse of Drugs Act	–	193
Other	138	209
Total	12,171	85,627

The Garda Commissioner's overview in his 1975 Report was bleak:

> "The overall crime picture can only be described as disturbing. Substantial increases in crime, first noted in 1966, have continued. Criminals are becoming more vicious and mean. Attacks on old and disabled people in their homes, a type of crime practically unknown in this country some years ago, are now on the increase. The use of firearms and other offensive weapons in robberies is becoming more widespread, and menacing."

By the early 1980s, the level of crime had reached unprecedented heights, and a peak of 102,400 indictable offences was recorded in 1983. After that, the crime level fell, but began to rise again during the 1990s to reach another peak of 102,500 in 1995. But then the crime level fell in 1996, and there were sharps fall in 1997 and 1998. Most of the fall in this period is explained by the sharp drop in robberies (including muggings), larceny (especially larceny from unattended vehicles) and burglaries.

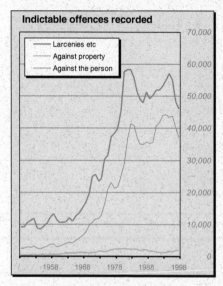

Between 1997 and 1998, crime in the Dublin area fell by 10%. In the same year, however, crime rose by over 10% in Cavan/Monaghan, and Roscommon/Galway East. In 1998, the highest crime rate was in Dublin North Central (147 indictable offences per 1,000 population). By contrast, the lowest was in Mayo (8 per 1,000).

Compared to 1949, crime in Ireland is now largely an urban problem, heavily concentrated in Dublin: 53% of all indictable offences in 1998 occurred in the Dublin region.

Despite the rise in crime, especially in the years up to 1983, the crime rate in Ireland is very low by EU standards. For example, the rate of homicide, crimes of violence and domestic burglary are all well below the EU average.

The table above compares the categories of indictable offences in 1949 and 1998. In some categories, there were fewer indictable offences in 1998 than in 1949. For example, Concealment of Birth (28 in 1949, 1 in 1998), Larceny of Pedal Cycles (1,420 to 292). In 1949, Attempting to Commit Suicide was still a crime (19 offences), though while proceedings were taken, convictions were rare.

Homicides in the period around 1949 were distributed fairly evenly in urban and rural areas. Moreover, they tended to occur within families. The pattern is now very different: they are more prevalent in the cities, and a much greater proportion occurs outside the family. The graph shows the numbers of deaths classified as murders, infanticides and non-traffic manslaughters. There were 15 such deaths in 1949. The corresponding figure for 1998 was 51. Of these, 41 were male and 10 female. The sudden peak in 1974 includes the 33 victims of the car bombs in Dublin and Monaghan in May of that year. The lowest year for homicides was 1963, when there were four murders and one manslaughter.

Armed robbery attracted much attention in 1949 because it was so unusual. There were only two cases, the most notable occurring in February when four young men entered an office and got away with £30 after striking a woman assistant with a revolver. By contrast, there were 88 armed robberies in 1997. More generally, the number of armed raids (robberies and aggravated burglaries involving firearms), also very low

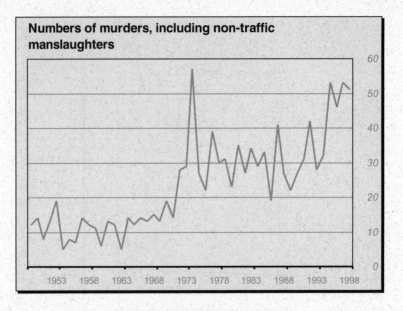

Numbers of murders, including non-traffic manslaughters

in 1949, increased sharply from the 1960s. It rose to 300 in 1971 and to almost 600 in 1981. In the space of only three years, to 1984, it doubled again to 1200. But after peaking at 1,400 in 1988, it began to fall. Between 1993 and 1998, it fell from 720 to 220. This fall has been particularly steep for armed raids on financial institutions.

The use of syringes in the course of criminal activity is a relatively recent phenomenon. The number of robberies and aggravated burglaries where syringes were used rose from 154 in 1993 to a peak of 1,104 in 1996, but then fell back to 442 in 1998.

As the 1990s progressed, indictable crime against tourists became an increasing problem. The number of crimes rose steadily to peak at just over 4,000 in 1996. By 1998, the number fell to 3,400. The vast bulk of these crimes take place in the Dublin region, and about 90% of them are larcenies.

The number of sexual assaults increased during the 1990s. There are problems of comparability over time because the reporting of such offences is considered to have increased and many reported offences had occurred years or decades previously. In 1998, 78% of the victims of indictable sexual assault were female. By contrast, 81% of the victims of indictable wounding and assault were male.

NON-INDICTABLE OFFENCES

As indicated earlier, the trend in the total number of offences should be treated with caution for various reasons. For example, in the Garda statistics up to 1993, the figures relate to the number of persons proceeded against for the various offences; for 1994 onwards, the statistics deal with the number of offences in which proceedings were taken.

Non-indictable offences (excluding drug offences)

	1949	1998
Assaults	1,200	8,800
Cruelty to animals	500	200
Firearms/Offensive Weapons Acts	200	1,600
Road Traffic Acts	97,900	238,200
Intoxicating Liquor Laws	16,800	15,700
Malicious/criminal damage	1,000	2,800
Vagrancy Acts	700	600
Other	46,700	145,500
Total	165,000	413,300

In both years, about 60% of offences are under the Road Traffic Acts. There were 97,900 such offences in 1949 and 238,200 in 1998. However, the distribution within this category is very different. In 1949, most traffic offences were under the Lighting Regulations, and most of these related to pedal cycles. The 1949 Garda Report on Crime lamented: "*Failure to carry lights on vehicles constitutes a serious danger to all road users, but in spite of advice and warnings issued by Gárda in most cases before prosecutions are entered, this form of offence continues to be prevalent throughout the whole country.*" In 1998, there were only 7,600 offences under the Lighting Regulations, and the most common traffic offences related to insurance (54,100), local bye-laws (51,600), driving licenses (39,200) and exceeding the speed limit (25,800). There were also 11,000 offences relating to dangerous/careless etc driving, 9,700 for not wearing a seat-belt, and 8,300 for drinking and driving. In the 1960s, there were very few drink-driving prosecutions, and most of those related to pedal cycles or horse-drawn vehicles.

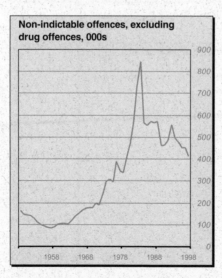

Non-indictable offences, excluding drug offences, 000s

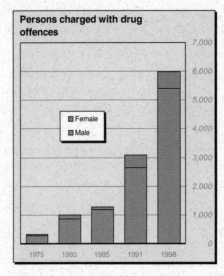

Persons charged with drug offences

The figures above exclude drug offences, which did not exist in 1949. The Drug Squad was formed in 1968. In 1971, 113 people were charged with drug offences. This almost doubled the following year, when offences relating to heroin began to appear. The numbers charged reached 1,000 in 1981 and 3,000 in 1991. Between 1996 and 1997 it nearly doubled to reach a peak of almost 8,000 before falling the following year to 6,000. 65% of cases were for possession and 30% for supplying or dealing. Half of the cannabis offences and virtually all of the heroin offences were recorded in the Dublin region.

The system of on the spot fines was introduced in 1963. The number of notices issued expanded very rapidly, and by 1969 had passed the 180,000 level. The number issued in 1998 was 357,000, of which 189,000 were for parking violations, 132,000 for speeding offences, and 36,000 for non-display of a licence disc. In most cases, the fines were paid and there were no court proceedings.

PRISONS AND PLACES OF DETENTION

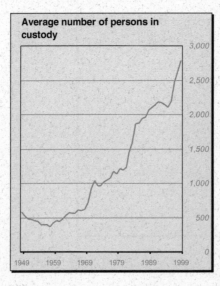

Average number of persons in custody

In 1949, the five prisons in order of size were Mountjoy (which held more than half of the prisoners in the State), Portlaoise, Limerick, Sligo, and Cork. With St Patrick's, Clonmel, there were six institutions in all. By 1999, the number of institutions had risen to 14. The new prisons included Wheatfield, Castlerea, Arbour Hill, Fort Mitchel on Spike Island and St. Patrick's Institution in Dublin.

By contrast with the 1990s, the Visiting Committees had few problems to deal with in 1949. They praised the food, the cleanliness and the hygiene. Their report for Mountjoy stated: "*Invariably, prisoners expressed satisfaction with their treatment, and no complaints were received during the year save one or two of a trivial nature which on investigation was unfounded.*" It was a mark of the times that the Minister for Justice granted certain remissions to prisoners serving sentences on Christmas Eve, 1949, "*to mark the beginning of the Holy Year and as an indication of the Government's complete harmony with the spirit of the Holy Season*". As a result, 143 prisoners were released and all others had their sentences reduced.

Daily average, prisons and other places of detention

	1949		1999 (first 8 months)	
	Male	Female	Male	Female
Mountjoy	270	47	753	61
Wheatfield	–	–	359	–
Cork	28	–	271	–
Limerick	50	12	214	14
St Patrick's Institution	–	–	198	–
Castlerea	–	–	189	–
Portlaoise	94	–	140	–
Arbour Hill	–	–	138	–
Fort Mitchel	–	–	101	–
Other	77	2	331	–
Total	519	61	2,694	75

The daily average prison population (including St Patrick's, Clonmel, for juveniles) was 580 in 1949. This fell to a low of 370 in 1958. After that, it began to rise, gradually at first but then more steeply. There were sharp rises in 1970-1972 and again in the early 1980s; in the 4-year period 1982-1985 alone, the average prison population rose by over 50%. There followed a decade or so of relatively modest increases, but the steep rise resumed in 1997.

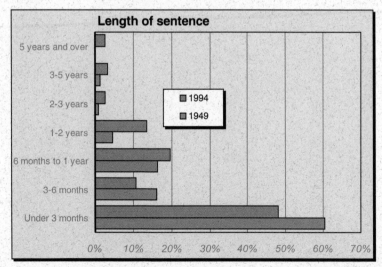

By European standards, Ireland has one of the highest proportions of prisoners aged under 21, — over a quarter. On the other hand, Ireland has a very low proportion of female prisoners — over 97% of the prison population is male. In 1994, there were 70 "lifers" in prison, all male, of which 65 were convicted for murder and 5 for rape.

A recent trend is the increase in the number of sexual offenders in prison. These men now form about one in eight of the prison population. Because of the nature of their offences, they tend to get long sentences.

As the graph shows, sentences are getting longer. A lower proportion gets sentences of 6 months or less, while a greater proportion gets longer sentences. The difference is particularly stark for long sentences — those of 5 years or over: in 1949, only 0.1% (one in a thousand) got 5 or more years; by 1994, this had risen to 2.6% (one in 40). Also, a greater proportion of those sentenced to prison consists of people in their 20s and 30s, and a far lower proportion of people aged 50 or over.

Give Him

Wolsey

Socks!

Choice of Ribbed and Plain.
Fine. Medium and Heavy.

·GIVE·HIM·WOLSEY·SOCKS·ALL·THE·YEAR·

Consumer Prices and Expenditure

Kevin McCormack, Peter Meany

INTRODUCTION

The Consumer Price Index (CPI), compiled and published each month by the CSO, is the official measure of inflation in Ireland. Since its inception in 1922, an extensive range of data on the prices of goods and services has been collected on a quarterly (and more recently on a monthly) basis. In addition to its primary role of providing an overall summary measure of price trends, the compilation of the CPI also enables us to track individual price changes for an extensive range of commodities.

The weights for the CPI are based on the results of the periodic Household Budget Surveys (HBS), which give us information on the average income and expenditure of private households. In addition to providing information on how the level of expenditure has been changing, the HBS also provides data on how the pattern of household expenditure has been changing over time.

THE "BASKET"

The selection of items for pricing — the "basket" — is made using the results of the national Household Budget Survey. The most recent HBS was for 1995 and covered the spending of a sample of 8,000 households. The 985 items in the current basket include not only the day to day items you would expect such as food, clothing, cars and petrol, but also items such as mobile telephones, medical insurance, bank charges, child-minding fees and mortgage interest repayments.

Expenditure weights from the HBS form a crucial component in the construction of the CPI. The weights from the 1995 HBS are summarised as follows.

CPI weights, November 1996

Commodity groups	%
Food	23
Alcohol	13
Tobacco	5
Clothing & footwear	6
Fuel & light	5
Housing	8
Household durables	4
Other goods	6
Transport	14
Services & related expenditure	17
Total all items	100

INFLATION OVER THE YEARS

Ireland's inflation rate is subject to international as well as domestic economic influence. It has varied considerably over the years. From the late 1940s to the early 1970s, prices rose at a modest level with the inflation rate fluctuating between 5% and 8%.

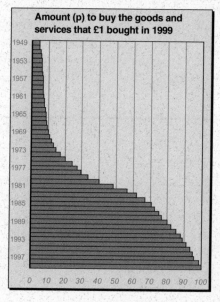

The period 1973 to 1988 was a time of high inflation. It reached an all-time high of 21% in 1975. As a result, over the 10-year period 1973 to 1983, price levels more than quadrupled.

The graph shows vividly how inflation has impacted on the purchasing power of money since 1949. In that year, less that 5p in today's money would have been sufficient to acquire the equivalent of £1 of goods and services at current prices.

Inflation fell rapidly since the mid-1980s and is now, by historic standards, very low. The last year in which inflation exceeded 5% was 1985.

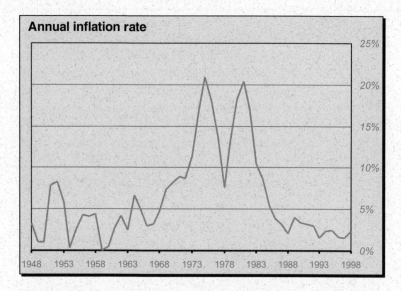

Annual inflation rate

Price trends vary for different groupings of goods and services.

Price increase for commodity groups

Group	Factor 1998/1968
Food	10.3
Alcohol	12.8
Tobacco	13.6
Clothing & footwear	5.8
Fuel & light	11.4
Housing	6.6
Household durables	6.9
Other goods	11.5
Transport	12.7
Services & related expenditure	14.0
All items	10.4

The table shows the factor by which prices have increased over the 30-year period from 1968 to 1998. Overall prices are now 10.4 times higher than at the start of the period. Prices for services, alcoholic drink, tobacco, transport and fuel have all increased faster than overall inflation. On the other hand, prices for clothing & footwear, housing and household durables have shown increases much lower than the overall rate. Food prices, despite significant fluctuations, have broadly increased in line with overall inflation.

Apart from index numbers, the CSO compiles and publishes comparable national average retail prices. Although they represent only a tiny proportion of the items priced for the CPI, they nevertheless make for interesting reading. One can compare average prices for some food items for the past fifty years and additional items since 1983. (National average prices for non-food items are available only since 1983.)

Comparable national average prices

Average prices	Unit	1949	1983	1999	Factor 1949/99	Factor 1983/99
Potatoes	Stone	14p	177p	480p	34	2.7
Sirloin steak	Pound	12p	278p	390p	33	1.4
Bread	Loaf	3p	42p	78p	26	1.9
Cheese	Pound	11p	139p	269p	25	1.9
Sugar	Pound	2p	27p	41p	21	1.5
Milk	Quart	3p	37p	72p	24	1.9
Butter	Pound	13p	83p	159p	12	1.9
Eggs	Eggs	17p	90p	147p	9	1.6
Draught stout	1 Pint	–	108p	216p	–	2.0
Cigarettes	20	–	127p	319p	–	2.5
Petrol	1 Litre	–	60p	62p	–	1.0

The table shows that a loaf of bread cost the equivalent of 3p in 1949 compared with 78p today, a 30-fold increase. Since the spending power of the £ in 1999 is about 21 times less than it was in 1949, this means that the price of bread (as well as sirloin steak and potatoes) has risen by much higher than the rate of inflation. By contrast, prices for eggs and butter have risen by much lower than the rate of inflation. If all items had risen by equal amounts, then eggs and butter would be about twice as dear as they are and potatoes would be a lot cheaper.

Between 1983 and 1998, prices rose by about 60%. Over this period, the price of butter, potatoes and cigarettes rose by much higher that the average, and the price of a pint of stout almost doubled. By contrast, the price of petrol was almost unchanged.

While not visible from the table, petrol is a striking example of how variable price trends for individual items can be over time. In the wake of the oil crises of the 1970s, the price more than doubled between 1973 and 1979, but despite some fluctuations has remained substantially unchanged since then.

The HBS enables the comparison of the expenditure patterns of house-holds across time. It is possible to compare the expenditure patterns of urban household from the very first HBS (1951-52) to the latest HBS (1994-95) and for all households (urban and rural) from 1973 to 1994-95.

Distribution of average weekly expenditure of urban households, %

	1951-52	1965-66	1980	1994-95
Food	37.6	31.5	25.5	21.4
Alcoholic	1.1	3.7	4.8	5.5
Tobacco	5.0	6.2	2.7	2.7
Clothing & footwear	13.0	9.1	8.7	6.4
Fuel & light	7.1	5.3	6.1	4.5
Housing	7.1	8.1	8.5	11.1
Household non-durables	1.1	1.6	1.9	2.3
Household durables	2.6	4.1	5.8	3.6
Miscellaneous goods	1.9	2.8	4.2	3.9
Transport	4.3	9.6	13.3	13.1
Services etc	19.2	18.0	18.5	25.6
Total expenditure	100.0	100.0	100.0	100.0

The table compares the percentage distribution of average weekly expenditure for urban household in selected surveys since 1951-52 to 1994-95, and shows the following trends:

- Expenditure over the period has steadily declined on essential items such as Food (from 37.6% to 21.4%) and Clothing & footwear (from 13% to 6.4%).

- For Alcoholic drink, expenditure rose quickly from 1.1% of house-hold expenditure in 1951-52 to 3.7% in 1965-66, and then at a moderate rate of 5.5% to 1994-95.

- Expenditure rose over the period for Housing (from 7.1 % to 11.1%) and Household non-durables (from 1.1% to 2.3%).

- Expenditure on Fuel and Light fluctuated over the period, and reached its lowest level in 1994-95 (4.5%).

- Expenditure on Transport rose steadily from 1951-52 (4.3%) to peak in 1980 (13.3%), decreasing slightly in 1994-95 (13.1%).

- Expenditure on Services rose sharply to 25.6% in 1994-95.

- Households were spending considerably less on Tobacco in 1994-95 then they did in 1951-52 (2.7% as compared to 5.0%).

The results of the surveys also allow us to look closely at the individual items within the main commodity groups. For example:

- In 1951-52, the consumption of pigs' heads and rabbits was very popular.

- Holiday expenditure in both 1951-52 and 1994-95 accounted for 3% of the household expenditure.

- Domestic service in 1951-52 accounted for approximately 2% of household expenditure, compared to 0.5% in 1994-95.

EXPENDITURE BY INCOME LEVELS

Another interesting feature of the HBS is the ability to look at the expenditure patterns of households with different income levels.

The graphs compare the percentage distribution of average weekly expenditure for households with high income (the top decile or 10% of households) and low income (the bottom decile) levels. High-income households spend far less of their income on Food, Tobacco (especially

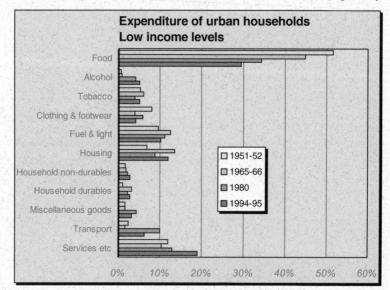

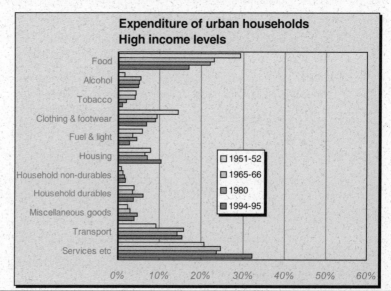

in 1994-95) and Fuel & light, and far more on Transport and Services.

Households with low income levels spent less on Food (29% in 1994-95 as compared to 52% in 1951-52) and Clothing & footwear (4% as compared to 8% in 1951-52) and are now spending more on Transport (6% as compared to 2% in 1951-52), Alcoholic drink (5% as compared to 1% in 1951-52) and Services (19% as compared to 12% in 1951-52). Expenditure on Tobacco changed relatively little, being about 5% of total expenditure.

If Food, Clothing & footwear, Fuel & light and Housing are the basic ingredients needed to live a normal life, then low income households now spend almost 21% less when compared to 1951-52 (56% as compared to 77%).

Households with high income levels spent less on Food (17% as compared to 29%) and Clothing & footwear (7% as compared to 14% in 1951-52) and are now spending more on Transport (16% as compared to 9% in 1951-52), Alcoholic drink (5% as compared to 2% in 1951-52) and Services (32% as compared to 21% in 1951-52). The above comparisons also show that high-income households are spending a lot less on Tobacco (1% as compared to 4% in 1951-52).

Taking the same basic elements as for low income households, the high-income households are now also spending 20% less when compared to 1951-52 (37% as compared to 57%).

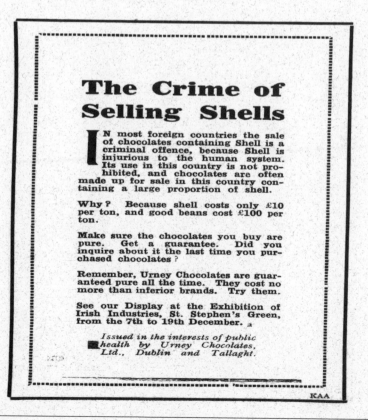

The Economy

John O'Hagan, Patrick Murphy, Adrian Redmond

INTRODUCTION

The economic development of the country in the past 50 years can be divided into several different periods. The single most dominant influence has probably been our membership of the European Union, which we joined, as the European Economic Community (the "Common Market") in 1973. As this date falls roughly half way through our period, it is convenient to use it as an intermediate year in several places in this chapter.

The basic measure of the level of economic activity in an economy is the Gross Domestic Product (GDP). This measures the value of the output of goods and services, or alternatively the income generated in the production of those goods and services, in the form of wages, profits etc.

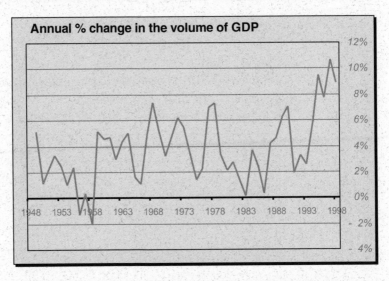

Annual % change in the volume of GDP

The GDP of the economy in 1998, at almost £60 billion, was about 150 times higher in value terms than in 1949. Most of this was, of course, due to inflation. Nevertheless, even in real terms (GDP at constant prices) output has multiplied by a net factor of about 6½, an annual average of about 3.8%. The growth, however, has not been uniform over these decades. The 1950s was a decade of relative stagnation, with actual reductions in output in two years towards the end of the decade. Modest growth in the early 1960s accelerated in the late 1960s and early 1970s, with the prospect of and achievement of accession to the EEC. The 1970s were erratic, with slowdowns brought about by the oil crises contrasting with two boom years in 1977 and 1978. The first half of the 1980s was again a period of stagnation. The solid growth that resumed in 1987 was briefly interrupted in the early 1990s, before taking off with remarkable vigour after 1993. The years 1994 to 1998 have seen the most sustained period of rapid growth in the whole period, giving rise to the label "The Celtic Tiger".

In the 23 years from 1949 until accession to the EEC, the total growth was about 2.1 times or an annual average of about 3.3%. In the 26 years since then, the growth has been about 3.1 times, or an annual average of about 4.4%. While it is clear that average annual growth since entry to the EEC has been somewhat higher, this is really a feature only since the mid-1980s, as much of the early boost expected from entry to the EEC was dissipated by the recurring oil crises of the 1970s and the budgetary crises of the early 1980s.

Although, as we have seen, the overall level of output increased by about 6½ times from 1949 to 1998, the population also increased by 25%. The net effect of this was that output per head was about 5.3 times higher in 1998 than in 1949.

GDP AND GNP

While GDP measures the value of goods and services produced in the economy, a better measure of the income that accrues to the residents of the economy is Gross National Product (GNP). This takes into account the fact that some of the income generated by production here is paid to foreigners, in the form of wages or dividends paid abroad, or interest

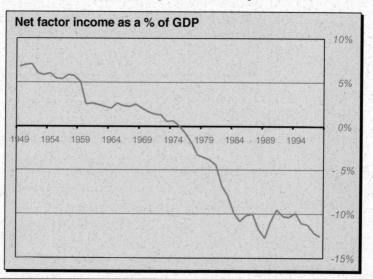

Net factor income as a % of GDP

paid to foreign lenders, while on the other hand, Irish residents may similarly benefit from such incomes paid from abroad.

Over the period since 1949, there has been a steady turnaround in this relationship. Up to the mid-1970s, we received more of these net factor incomes from abroad than we paid out. In the 1950s, for example, GNP was on average 5.9% higher than GDP. However the increasing scale of the national debt (and in particular the proportion owed to foreigners), the rise in interest rates in the 1970s and 1980s, and especially the vast expansion of profits earned by foreign-owned companies in Ireland, have reversed the position. In the 1990s, on average, GNP is some 11% short of GDP. This difference is by far the highest in the EU except for

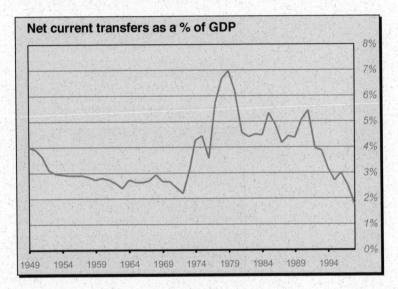

Net current transfers as a % of GDP

Luxembourg (which is a special case because of its role as a financial centre).

An even wider concept is Gross National Disposable Income, which also reflects net flows of transfer incomes (gifts, subsidies, taxes) with the rest of the world. Throughout our period, Ireland has been a net recipient of such flows. As a percentage of GDP, the net benefit to the country has always been greater than 2.2%, apart from the rapid decline to 1.7% in 1998, and has been as high as 7.0% (in 1979).

However, the source and nature of these transfers has changed radically. In the early phase, one of the larger components was emigrants' remittances, mainly from Britain and the United States. At the start of the period, these added about 2.7% to GDP, and still averaged about 1.6% in the 1960s, but their impact now is relatively trivial. Entry to the EEC transformed the picture completely, and agricultural subsidies and the European Social Fund have replaced emigrants' remittances as the main source of net transfers. (For more details, see the Balance of Payments section later in this chapter.)

THE STRUCTURE OF THE ECONOMY

Agriculture accounted for about 31% of output in 1949, and food production accounted for a substantial proportion of the 26% of output due to manufacturing industry. Other branches of manufacturing industry were based in the main on traditional technologies and on the pre-war environment of protection from foreign competition by tariffs and quotas. By 1998, agriculture had shrunk to just 5% of output, and Ireland had become a modern advanced economy. Industry accounted for 38% of the output in that year, and there has been a decisive shift away from traditional low-technology sectors. The share of services, at 57%, is still rising, although still a few percentage points short of the 60 to 65% share typical of the most advanced Western European countries (or the 70% of the United States).

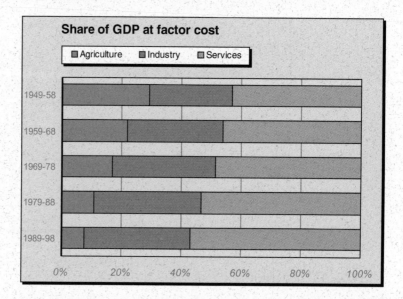

The evolution away from dependence on agriculture has been more or less continuous over the half century. For the first two decades or so, industry was the main source for the increased share, but the shift towards services has been decisive in recent decades.

WAGE EARNERS AND PROFIT EARNERS

The relative shares of income accruing to wage and salary earners and to profit earners have varied considerably during the period. In general, the share going to profit earners (companies and self-employed persons, including farmers and professionals) tends to increase during periods of rapid growth, but some longer term trends are also present.

The profit share has always been less than the wage share, but for most of the period it has been below the high levels seen at the beginning of the period (over 80% of the wages amount in 1949). From the mid-

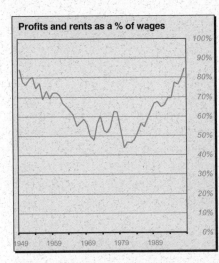

Profits and rents as a % of wages

1950s, the profit share entered on a long period of decline, briefly arrested in the mid-1970s, after accession to the EEC boosted farmers' incomes. By 1980, profits amounted to only 44% of wages. The recovery that followed has been rather more rapid than the long slow decline, with the increasing profitability of foreign-owned companies having a major effect. In the 1990s, in particular, the growth of profits has been spectacular, and the half-century ends as it began, with aggregate incomes in the form of profits again at over 80% of wages. The composition has of course changed dramatically: in the 50s, agriculture accounted for almost 60% of profits; by the end of the century it has been completely overtaken by manufacturing and services companies (many of them foreign-owned) and by other forms of self-employment.

EXPENDITURE COMPONENTS OF GDP AND THE EXPORTS BOOM

In addition to describing the economy in terms of sectors and income types, it is also interesting to look at the expenditure categories of GDP. These are the classic macro-economic textbook concepts of Private consumption, Government consumption, Investment, Exports and Imports. The following chart illustrates how the composition of GDP has varied over the period.

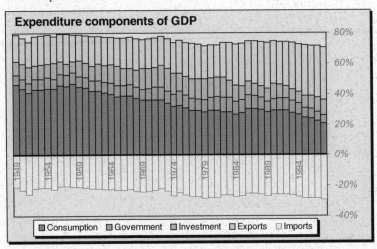

Perhaps the most significant feature is the decline in the relative importance of private consumption, from around 80% of GDP at the mid-century to just over 50% now. Government consumption has accounted for a small part of this long-term shift, having risen from 11 to 13% (although it had risen much higher in the middle part of the period, peaking at about 20% in the early 1980s). Investment, which tends to be much more cyclical than the other components, has risen substantially over the long term, from 16% to about 24% by end-century, having been as high as 30% or more in some years in the 1970s and early 1980s. After falling back substantially in the late 1980s and early 1990s, with the cutbacks in government investment in the years of budgetary crisis having a dramatic effect, investment activity has boomed in the 1990s, with construction experiencing unprecedented levels.

Over the full span of the half-century, however, the single most dramatic change has been the expansion of exports and, to a lesser extent, of imports of goods and services. The economy was reasonably open even in the early part of our period, in the arithmetical sense that exports and imports were sizeable, even if the trading and customs regime were still heavily affected by residual wartime controls, tariffs and quotas. By the end of the century, however, it has become one of the most open economies in Europe.

At the outset, exports were about 30% of GDP, and imports about 36 to 40%. These ratios more or less marked time during the stagnant 1950s as a whole, albeit with some individual years where the import excess widened dramatically, but both began to rise steadily from the early 1960s, due partly to the liberalising effect of the Anglo-Irish Free Trade Agreement of 1965. The growth of exports began to outpace that of imports, although the consequent reduction in the import excess was interrupted by the price rises for oil and other commodities during the oil crises of the 1970s. The surge in exports gathered increasing strength in the late 1970s, based on access to the EEC agricultural and industrial markets. By the mid-1980s exports finally exceeded imports, and the export-led boom has powered ahead, leading to the remarkable levels being achieved in the final years of the century, with exports in excess of 80% of GDP. The substantial import excess of the early years has been comprehensively reversed due to the expansion of merchandise trade, although there is a large and growing deficit on services. The development of merchandise trade is worth a closer look.

MERCHANDISE TRADE

The period after the war was a time of rationing and strict controls. Exports and imports were still heavily regulated through Government Orders made under Emergency Powers legislation. There was a ban on the exports of certain products, and others could only be exported under licence, or could only be exported to particular countries. Imports were controlled using quotas and some very high rates of Customs Duty. In 1949, Ireland's external trade was slowly recovering from the effects of the war. Imports were rising rapidly; exports were rising at a more modest rate and, in volume terms, were still far below the volume of exports in the pre-war years. As a result, the trade deficit was increasing rapidly: the value of our imports was more than double the value of our exports.

The post-war recovery of Germany could be seen in the trade statistics. Imports from Germany, at £0.5m in 1949, were three times what they

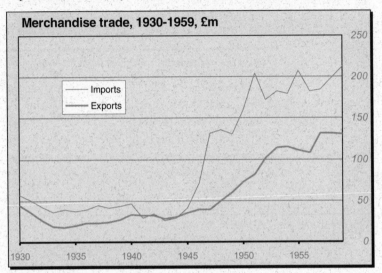

Merchandise trade, 1930-1959, £m

were the previous year, but they were to be ten times greater again by 1951. Similar changes could be observed in our trade with Austria and Japan. Further post-war effects could be seen in our imports of wheat and maize. We imported huge amount of wheat in 1948 from Argentina and Australia; the following year not a single grain of wheat was imported from these countries — it all came from the USA and Canada. Similarly, in 1948 we imported over 200,000 tonnes of maize, all of it from Argentina; in the next year, nearly all of our imports of maize was from the USA.

TRADE IN THE LATE 1940S

Our exports were dependent on agriculture, and we were also heavily dependent on the UK. In 1949, 91% of Ireland's exports went to the UK. This was followed by the Netherlands at 2.4%, Belgium at 2.1%, and the USA who got less than 1% of our exports. Our high dependency on agriculture for our foreign earnings is shown by the fact that £44m of our £61 exports were of live animals and food. The exports of these products to the UK alone accounted for more than two-thirds of our exports.

Products traded in 1949

Exports	%	Imports	%
Cattle	34.7	Coal	5.5
Horses†	9.3	Maize	4.2
Fresh hen eggs	8.9	Horses†	2.6
Ale, beer, porter	7.5	Wheat	2.6
Chocolate crumb	3.0	Raw tobacco	2.6
Dead turkeys	2.2	Tea	2.4
Tinned beef	1.9	Deals, planks, boards	2.2

† Most of this was temporary trade for racing or breeding.

Imports in 1949 were a lot less concentrated than exports. Of the total of £130m imported, 57% originated in the UK and 14% in the USA. We imported substantial amounts of textiles, electrical goods, vehicles, coal, cereals, raw tobacco, timber and tea. We also imported 10,000 electric vacuum cleaners, 23,000 second-hand overcoats, as well as a surprisingly large amount of motor spirit form the Dutch West Indies.

TRADE IN THE LATE 1990S

After a half a century, Ireland's trade pattern was dramatically different. Instead of massive deficits, the balance showed a strong and expanding surplus. While the UK was still our main trading partner, it now accounts for only a third of our imports and a quarter of our exports. Our other main trading partners were, in order, the USA, Germany, France, the Netherlands, Japan, Belgium/Luxembourg, and Singapore (from whom we imported over £1.5 billion in 1998).

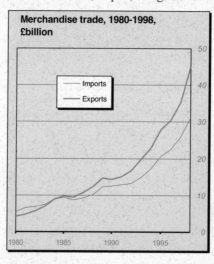

Merchandise trade, 1980-1998, £billion

The other main change is apparent from the products in which we traded: while we exported almost £2 billion of meat and dairy products in 1998, this was only 4% of total exports. Instead of consisting of basic commodities like cattle, eggs, beer, coal and tea, Ireland's trade is now dominated by the industrial materials, components, plant and products of multinational corporations, notably computer equipment, electrical machinery, and chemical and pharmaceutical products.

Products traded in 1998

Exports	%
Computer equipment	22.4
Organic chemicals	17.3
Electrical machinery	7.5
Medical & pharmaceutical products	7.4
Oils, perfumes, etc	3.5
Telecommunications equipment	3.0
Meat & meat preparations	2.5
Scientific apparatus, etc	2.4

Imports	%
Computer machinery	19.9
Electrical machinery	11.0
Road vehicles	7.0
Organic chemicals	3.1
Telecommunications equipment	2.9
General industrial machinery	2.8
Medical & pharmaceutical products	2.3
Petroleum, etc	1.9

BALANCE OF PAYMENTS

As with most countries, merchandise trade has been the dominant influence on Ireland's balance of payments (BoP) with the rest of the world in the half century. The move from deficit to surplus on trade in goods has resulted in a parallel movement from deficit to surplus in the overall balance on current account. But there are several other ways in which a country receives from or pays for services and incomes vis-à-vis foreigners. Over the half century some of these have been quite significant for Ireland, and their relative importance has varied considerably.

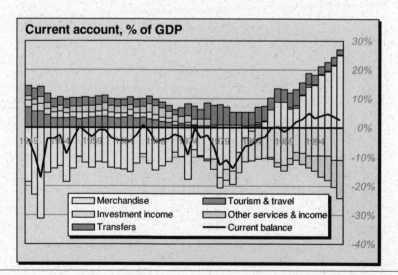

Current account, % of GDP

Legend: Merchandise, Investment income, Transfers, Tourism & travel, Other services & income, Current balance

The first graph shows the balances on the five categories of the current account, expressed as percentages of GDP. The overall BoP current account balance is also shown (the heavy line). As can be seen, there was only a slight improvement in the goods deficit in the long period up to the early 1980s, followed by a rapid and accelerating move into surplus since then. The aggregate of the so-called "invisibles" items (services, investment income and transfers) behaved in more or less the opposite way. These were generally positive up until the early 1980s, but have turned negative overall since then. However the balance on merchandise usually dominated, with the net effect that the BoP current account was in surplus in only a few years until the mid-1980s, but has been consistently in surplus since then.

A closer look at the individual components is rather revealing. As we have seen, the scale of goods trade has expanded dramatically. The

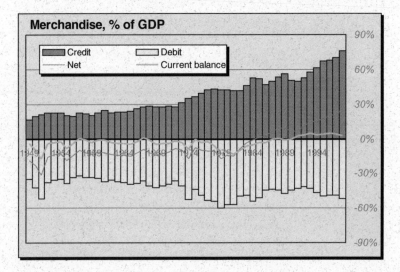

graph shows that until the mid-1970s imports were around 35 to 40% of GDP in most years, and exports grew slowly from about 20% to about 30%. Both have expanded greatly since then, but the export growth has outpaced the import growth, resulting in the move into surplus in the mid-1980s and the fast-growing surplus since then.

Tourism is now much less significant (relative to GDP) than it was in the early years. In the very early years it was of great importance, contributing a positive balance of 5% or 6% of GDP, and still positive to the tune of 3% or more as late as 1969. From the early 1970s exports (revenue from visitors to Ireland) dropped off rapidly, while increasing prosperity allowed Irish people to take more foreign holidays, with the result that the surplus balance on tourism had all but disappeared by the 1980s. Although absolute flows have increased substantially in both directions since then, the net effect, relative to the overall growth of GDP, has been relatively modest.

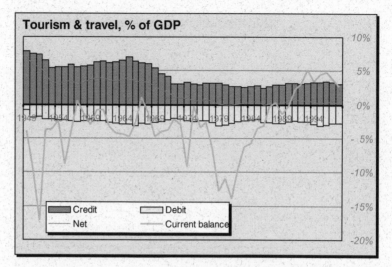

Tourism & travel, % of GDP

The evolution of investment income has been rather more dramatic. Inflows (interest earned by Irish residents on deposits and loans to foreign banks etc, and profits and dividends received from shareholdings in foreign companies) have been of the order of 4% to 5% of GDP throughout most of the period, although the increasing openness to international financial traffic in the 1990s has resulted in a substantial upturn in recent

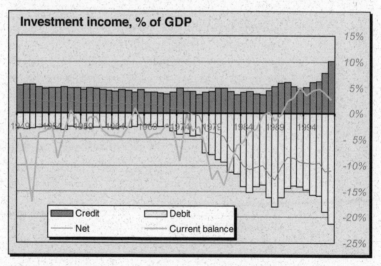

Investment income, % of GDP

years. Outflows were consistently less than inflows until about the mid-1970s, but have substantially outstripped the inflows ever since then. At the most extreme, at the end of the 1980s, the deficit on investment income was almost 13% of GDP. While profit and dividend outflows have continued to increase since then, the fall in interest rates and the reduction in the share of the national debt owed to foreigners in the 90s has had a beneficial effect, and the deficit balance fell back to around 9% in the mid-1990s, picking up again to about 11% by the end of the decade as the scale of profit outflows by multinationals continues to increase.

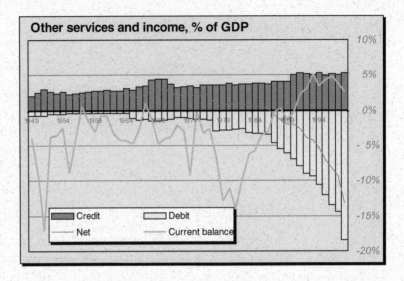

Other services and income, % of GDP

The miscellaneous category of other services and income has assumed enormous importance in recent years. In the earlier part of the period it covered a mixed bag, including such items as transportation services, postal and telecommunications services, government services, business services and earnings of Irish people temporarily working abroad, and was usually in modest surplus. In most years until the late 1980s, neither inflows nor outflows exceeded 4% of GDP, and inflows were consistently higher. However from the late 1970s the debit (outflows) side started to increase rapidly, mainly due to the very rapid expansion in payments by foreign-owned companies to their parents and other affiliates abroad for inter-company services and in the form of royalties on production processes. This, together with the profit outflows, have gone a large way to reduce the net effect of the merchandise surplus, much of which was of course also due to the same companies. The two effects have expanded dramatically in the 1990s, with the effect that by the end of the period, the balance on these other services and income is a deficit of around 13% of GDP.

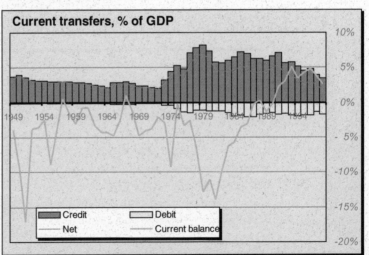

Current transfers, % of GDP

The final component of the current account of the balance of payments is current transfers. Here the story is uniformly good news. Throughout the period we have always been in the fortunate position of receiving more then we paid out, and the balance has been quite significant. For several decades the biggest component was emigrants' remittances, and these contributed substantially to the positive balance of about 3% of GDP in the 1950s and even into the 1960s. But the net effect was declining slowly, and by the time of entry to the Common Market the balance was down to less than 2%. The transfers from Brussels changed the picture dramatically after 1972, with the balance peaking at 7% of GDP in 1979. The main components of this were the agricultural subsidies and the receipts from the Social Fund programmes for combating unemployment and educational shortfalls. By the mid-1990s, however, the effect of the EU current transfers was declining, and Ireland's own contributions to the EU budget were beginning to rise as a result of our increasing prosperity. We end the period with net current transfers right back to their pre-EU level at just less than 2% of GDP.

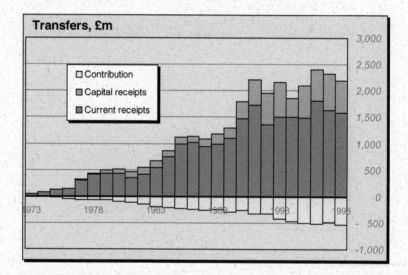

In addition to current EU transfers, we have also of course received large volumes of capital transfers under the regional fund and the cohesion fund schemes. While these are not reckoned in the BoP current account balance, they have of course been very substantial and have contributed significantly to the development of the productive capacity of the economy. Over the whole period since 1973, Ireland has received around £30bn from the EU. About £23bn of this has been in the form of current transfers (with agriculture accounting for about £20bn of this), and over £6bn has been capital in nature. Our contribution to the EU budget has been almost exactly equal to the capital transfers receipts, at a little over £6bn.

HOW MANY ZEROES?

What price the 100 billion economy? If we cheat a little, and measure our GDP in our new Euro currency, we can see that we are heading rapidly towards the 100 billion mark. The 1998 GDP of about 60 billion Irish pounds looks even more impressive in euros at around 76 billion. Even if inflation continues at its present modest levels, a few more years of growth at the sort of rate we have been experiencing in the 1990s will rapidly bring us up to the magic 100. By the time the pound disappears from the scene in 2002, will we have to add an extra digit to our tables? And when our successors come to write the 100th anniversary edition in 2049, what currency will they be using, and with how many zeroes?

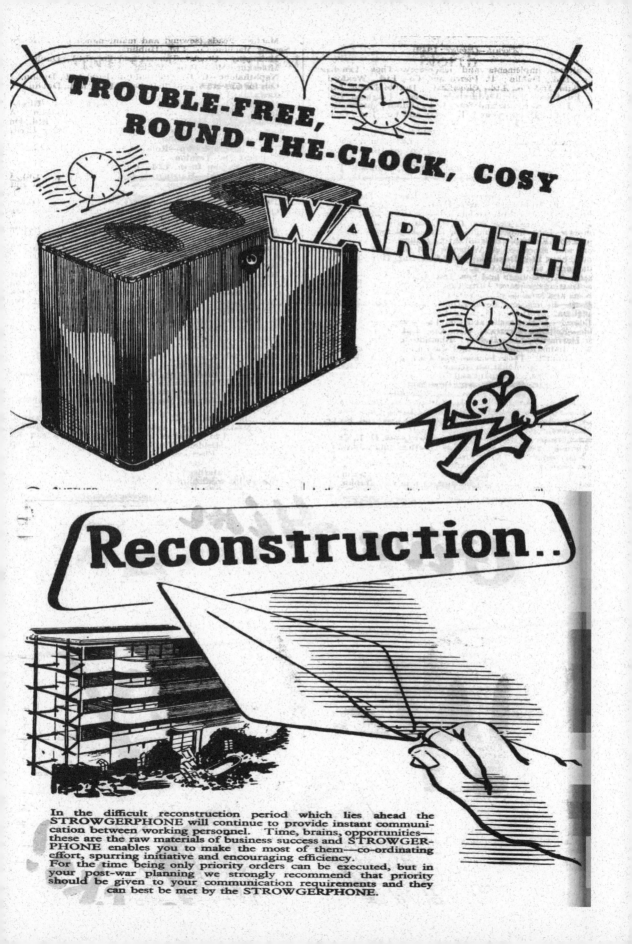

TROUBLE-FREE, ROUND-THE-CLOCK, COSY WARMTH

Reconstruction..

In the difficult reconstruction period which lies ahead the STROWGERPHONE will continue to provide instant communication between working personnel. Time, brains, opportunities— these are the raw materials of business success and STROWGERPHONE enables you to make the most of them—co-ordinating effort, spurring initiative and encouraging efficiency.

For the time being only priority orders can be executed, but in your post-war planning we strongly recommend that priority should be given to your communication requirements and they can best be met by the STROWGERPHONE.

Manufacturers of

WOOLLENS AND WORSTEDS, SERGES, BLANKETS & RUGS

TRADE ONLY SUPPLIED

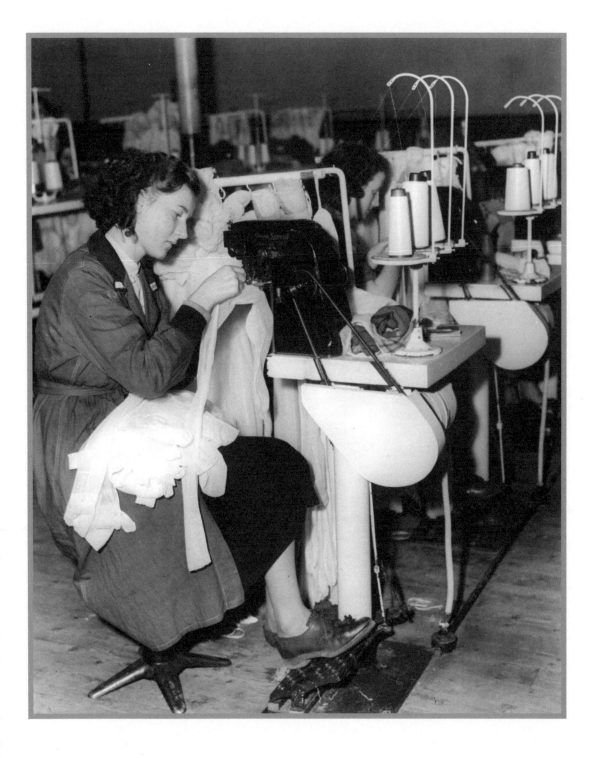

Labour Market

Joe Treacy, Norma O'Connell

1946: EVERY PICTURE TELLS A STORY

Fifty years ago, statisticians did not have computers at their disposal. Graphs such as these, which appeared in *The Trend of Employment and Unemployment* in 1951, were drawn by hand.

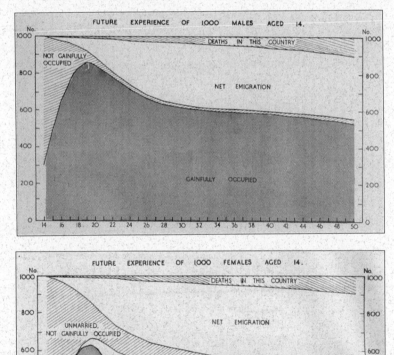

They portrayed the likely future experience of 1,000 males and females aged 14 in 1946, up to the age of 50, using the latest data then available on emigration, marriage, mortality and the labour force. In a sense, this was a precursor to the CSO's subsequent population and labour force projections. There were earlier forecasts. In 1935, R C Geary (who was to become the first Director of the CSO in 1949) predicted, in a paper entitled *The Future Population of Saorstát Éireann and Some Observations on Population Statistics* (in the *Journal of the Statistical and Social Inquiry Society of Ireland*, Vol. XV, 1934-1935) that the population of Ireland was "unlikely to exceed 3,700,000 during the next 80 years". His prediction for the total figure held true for the following 63 years, and only in 1998 did the population increase to over 3.7 million. The graphs in the 1951 *Trend* illustrated how things would turn out over the next 36 years if current patterns continued. So, what story did these graphs tell? How well did the forecasts turn out?

The graphs reflected some harsh realities of the times. Mortality was higher (and life expectancy shorter) in the 1950s. Only 90% of the imaginary cohort were expected to live beyond the age of 50, whereas today about 95% of boys and 97% of girls aged 14 can expect to reach at least their 50th birthday. Life expectancy for children born in 1996, at around 73 years for boys and almost 79 years for girls, was a considerable improvement on the 1950s. Indeed, with the continuing advances in medical science, today's young people can look forward on average to even greater longevity.

As many as 30% of males and 40% of females were expected to emigrate, most before the age of 30. The men and women who remained would have very different lifetime experience of the labour force. The majority of men were expected to be gainfully occupied. However, a much lower percentage of women would remain in the labour force after their early 30s. The career options available to women were fewer and, in general, women left their jobs when they married. The label "not gainfully occupied", which applied to those women who married and became homemakers, looks quaint today!

In 1971, Brendan Walsh included an updated version of this graph in a paper *Aspects of labour supply and demand with special reference to the employment of women in Ireland* (in the *Journal of the Statistical and Social Inquiry Society of Ireland*, Vol. XXII, Part III, 1970-1971), that anticipated how topical an issue women's involvement in the labour market was to become. The data for the years 1961 to 1966, which he used as a starting point, showed that mortality had improved considerably, that there was lower emigration, and that the marriage rate had increased. There was also a moderate increase in the proportion of women "gainfully occupied" across all age groups. However, greater changes were just around the corner.

50 YEARS LATER: HOW THINGS TURNED OUT

The 14-year olds of 1946 would have reached their 50th birthdays by 1982. Various CSO figures will tell us how things actually turned out for that age group. About 570,000 babies were born in Ireland in the 1930s. However, the 1981 Census figures recorded just 313,000 people who were born in the 1930s. Among the many factors that affect the comparison of these two figures, one thing in particular is clear: the massive toll taken by emigration in the 1950s.

Broadly speaking, the graphs predicted subsequent population and labour force trends quite well. However, there were some details they did not predict. The right-hand portion of the graph for females would have suggested that, by the early 1980s, no more than a fifth of women in their forties would be in the labour force. In fact, about a quarter of women aged between 45 and 54 were in the labour force in 1981. The overall census results for that year showed that 76% of men and just under 30% of women were in the labour force. Women's participation in the workforce has grown considerably since then and the total number of jobs in the economy has scaled new peaks.

TRANSITION FROM A MAINLY AGRICULTURAL ECONOMY

Ireland in the late 1940s was still very much a rural economy. More than half the men and about a quarter of the women in the labour force were involved in agriculture. In total, almost 600,000 people had agricultural occupations as proprietors, relatives assisting or as employees. There were more than 100,000 agricultural labourers, about a quarter of them living in.

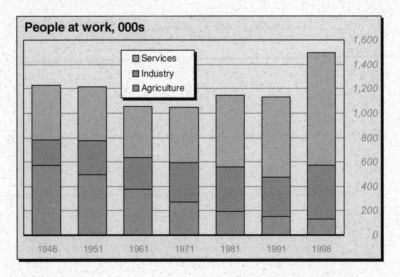

Total employment fell back considerably in the 1950s and remained more or less on a plateau through much of the 1960s. The workforce fell from about 1,228,000 in 1946 to 1,053,000 in 1961; and the level of employment in 1971 was not much different from 1961. After the mixed fortunes of the 1970s and 1980s, the fastest growth ever in Ireland's labour force has taken place during the 1990s. The bar chart shows the transition from agriculture towards more industrial employment in the 1960s and the substantial growth in the services sector which has provided the bulk of the latest growth in the labour force.

OCCUPATIONS SEGREGATED BY SEX

Men and women gainfully occupied, by occupation, 1946

Occupation (persons)

	Male	Female	Total
Agriculture & fishing occupations	516,000	82,000	597,000
Mining, quarrying, turf workers	3,000	–	3,000
Other production workers	152,000	35,000	188,000
Transport and communications	58,000	1,000	59,000
Commerce and finance	56,000	32,000	88,000
Public administration and defence	35,000	8,000	43,000
Professions	34,000	37,000	71,000
Personal service occupations	21,000	102,000	123,000
Clerks	20,000	24,000	44,000
Other occupations	68,000	15,000	83,000
Total gainfully occupied	964,000	335,000	1,298,000

Occupation (% distribution)

	Male	Female
Agriculture & fishing occupations	86%	14%
Mining, quarrying, turf workers	99%	1%
Other production workers	81%	19%
Transport and communications	98%	2%
Commerce and finance	64%	36%
Public administration and defence	82%	18%
Professions	48%	52%
Personal service occupations	17%	83%
Clerks	45%	55%
Other occupations	82%	18%
Total gainfully occupied	74%	26%

The table shows the broad allocation of jobs between men and women in 1946, just three years before the CSO was founded. The figures relate to persons who were gainfully occupied (at work or unemployed).There were almost three times as many men gainfully occupied as there were women. Jobs in agriculture, manufacturing, transport, communication and storage and in commerce, insurance and finance were occupied mainly by men. The largest occupational category for women was personal services, with 79,000 women employed as domestic servants. This category subsequently fell dramatically.

In general, women's participation was mainly confined to younger age groups and to a restricted number of occupations. Even in occupational groups where the table would suggest at least equality in terms of numbers, there was clear segregation by sex. For example, over 30,000 of the 37,000 women in the professions were in just three occupations: nuns, nurses and teachers.

INCREASE IN FEMALE PARTICIPATION

The changes in female labour force participation in the past 50 years can reasonably be categorised into three phases: pre-1971; the twenty years from 1971 to 1991; and the more recent years of rapid economic growth.

Women in the labour force, 000s

During the 1970s women's participation in the labour force began to grow. Much of this phase of growth was associated with the abolition of the marriage bar for women in public service jobs. Between 1971 and 1991 the number of women in the workforce grew by 100,000. In the next six years, the number of women at work grew by over 120,000 to reach 512,800 by 1997.

The long-term growth in the labour force and population can be seen in the table, which shows the numbers of men and women in the various Principal Economic Status (PES) categories, in selected years between 1971 and 1997. The choice of years in this table is somewhat arbitrary and a closer look at some of the intervening years would, of course, show the impact on both employment and unemployment of economic setbacks as well as the long-term trends.

Apart from the increase in female labour force participation, the number of men in the labour force also grew over the period shown, with 52,000 more men classified as at work and 68,000 more unemployed in 1997 than in 1971. However, the level of male participation in the labour force has not grown in line with the growth in the overall population.

Persons aged 15 or over classified by Principal Economic Status (000)

	1971	1987	1991	1997
Male				
At work	773.9	735.5	747.3	825.6
Unemployed	62.1	176.5	155.9	130.6
Student	69.9	131.0	146.2	176.1
Home duties	3.5	5.5	7.0	9.2
Retired	†	148.9	163.8	179.5
Other	110.6	52.4	50.4	62.0
Total	1,020.0	1,249.8	1,270.6	1,383.1
Female				
At work	275.6	354.9	386.3	512.8
Unemployed	13.8	55.6	52.8	48.3
Student	67.0	129.6	145.7	181.9
Home duties	634.9	670.8	645.8	588.0
Retired	†	44.1	53.9	66.2
Other	35.8	27.4	30.1	34.8
Total	1,027.1	1,282.3	1,314.6	1,432.0

† In 1971, retired people were included in the category "Other".

The proportion of women describing their economic situation as on "home duties" has been falling steadily: from 62% in 1971 to 53% in 1987, 49% in 1991, and 41% in 1997. There were 588,000 women in this category in 1997 compared with 635,000 in 1971. As we will see later, many more women today combine family and workplace commitments. Another important trend to which we will return is longer continuation in education. In 1997, there were 358,000 students aged 15 and over — an increase of more than 220,000 in just over a quarter century; just over half the students were female.

The ILO labour force classification provides a breakdown between full-time and part-time employment since the 1980s. Increasing part-time employment has been a feature of labour force growth. Between 1987 and 1997, the number of women in full-time jobs grew by about 102,000 and part-time by 68,000. The total increase of 170,000 over the ten years is greater than indicated in the PES table above for the number of women describing themselves as at work. The ILO classification, which is based on questions about actual labour market participation, gives a more comprehensive picture of women's employment.

WORK AND THE FAMILY

Using the ILO classification, we can also look at how women's employment and family commitments interact. The table shows that the number of working mothers almost doubled in the ten years from 1987, reaching 235,300 in 1997. Some 75,000 working mothers had just one dependent child, 79,800 had two dependent children, and 59,300 had three or more dependent children. There were large but less dramatic increases in the number of wives or partners without children in employment (+35,000) and the number of other females in employment (+20,500).

Females aged 15 and over: employment and labour force participation

Family situation	Employment (000)		Participation rate	
	1987	1997	1987	1997
Wives/partners without children	44.9	79.9	34.0%	43.1%
Mothers	120.6	235.3	26.5%	42.1%
Number of dependent children:				
None	9.4	20.8	14.3%	22.8%
1	36.9	75.3	33.1%	47.5%
2	36.9	79.8	31.5%	50.3%
3 or more	37.4	59.3	22.9%	39.0%
Other females	204.0	224.5	44.7%	41.6%
15-24	109.3	99.5	51.1%	40.4%
25-64	90.1	120.7	69.9%	73.9%
65 or over	4.7	7.2	3.7%	3.2%
Total in employment	369.5	539.7	35.0%	42.0%

The table also shows how the ILO labour force participation rate (the percentage who are in the labour force) has evolved. This grew from 35% in 1987 to 42% in 1997. In 1987, just over a quarter of mothers were in the labour force, considerably below the overall participation rate for females. In 1997, however, there was very little difference between the labour force participation of mothers and of other women.

The number of dependent children had some effect on labour force participation. Mothers with no dependent children (those with grown-up children in jobs and still living in the family home) had lower labour force participation than mothers currently raising their families. Younger mothers with three or more dependent children were considerably less likely to be in the labour force than those with one or two dependent children.

A more detailed analysis shows a higher percentage of working mothers in part-time employment: 36% compared with 13% for all other women in employment in 1997. A breakdown by age categories shows that participation rates increased between 1987 and 1997 in all age groups above 25 but fell for the under 25s. This reflects longer continuation in full-time education. Labour force participation is highest, at about 90%, for women aged 25 to 34 who do not have children and is relatively lower in the higher age groups.

IMPACT OF FREE EDUCATION

The table presents a snapshot of the educational profile of the population aged 15 to 64, excluding students, in 1997. Overall, 22% of people had completed education to primary level, about 56% had completed second level and 22% third level. About half of people aged 55 or over had primary education and over one third have completed secondary education. For those aged 45 to 54, the percentages are the other way round, with about one third educated to primary level and half having secondary education. So, during the 1950s and 1960s, people were leaving school at a later age.

Persons aged 15 to 64 by highest level of education completed, 1997

	Total	Primary	Secondary	Third level
Male	1,012,000	20%	57%	23%
Female	1,028,000	24%	54%	22%
Total	2,041,000	22%	56%	22%
15-19	71,000	14%	81%	5%
20-24	226,000	8%	64%	28%
25-29	259,000	8%	59%	33%
30-34	261,000	11%	61%	28%
35-39	257,000	13%	62%	25%
40-44	245,000	20%	58%	22%
45-49	228,000	32%	51%	17%
50-54	198,000	39%	46%	16%
55-59	156,000	45%	41%	14%
60-64	140,000	53%	35%	12%
In employment	1,325,000	14%	57%	30%
Unemployed	154,000	29%	60%	11%
Not in labour force	562,000	40%	52%	8%

In the 40 to 44 age group, the percentage having completed second level is appreciably higher, at 58%, and over a fifth had completed third level education. This is the first age group to have benefited from the introduction of free secondary education at the end of the 1960s. All younger age groups also gained. One third of those aged 25 to 29 had third level education, 59% had secondary education, and just over 8% had completed only primary education. The figures for the under 25s do not give the final picture, as they exclude those who have yet to complete their education.

Some 30% of those in employment in 1997 had third level education. A similar percentage of the unemployed had primary education whereas just 11% had completed third level education. The emerging picture is of demand for a labour force with ever-higher qualifications.

CONCLUSION

Many of the statistics we have presented in this chapter are taken from the Labour Force Surveys conducted by the CSO since 1975. These annual surveys were superseded at the end of 1997 by the new Quarterly National Household Survey, which promises to deliver more frequent and more detailed information about the labour force and social conditions generally. The statistical tools available when the CSO was founded 50 years ago were fewer, and blunter. Labour Force Surveys were in existence only in a few countries. In Ireland, statistics on employment were gathered in a variety of sector-specific employer surveys; the main sources were the June agricultural enumerations and the Census of Industrial Production. The five-yearly Census of Population was the only source of data on both employment and unemployment. Although the statistical techniques may have advanced in the meantime, it is interesting to note that some of the conceptual questions are very similar.

The use of the Live Register as a monthly unemployment indicator was as hotly debated then as it has been in the more recent past. An article in the *Trend of Employment and Unemployment* in 1935 noted that the description "Live Register of the Unemployed" was "seriously misleading", and many articles referred to the impact on the figures of administrative changes. Notes such as these, about what the Live Register figures actually mean, bear a remarkable resemblance to some commentaries written in the 1990s.

We began this chapter by looking back on past statisticians' efforts at forecasting. We may have been a little unfair to them. After all, we have the benefit of hindsight. We also have more detailed data sources at our disposal and a vastly different technology to analyse data. Inevitably, we see things from a different perspective. No doubt, anybody who looks back on the CSO 50 years from now will see the continuity of some ideas but will also, like us looking back on the CSO at its foundation, see some of today's figures from very different perspectives.

Fit for Kings

King Edward Potatoes - and your own
products - need the best packing you can give them.

Agriculture, Forestry and Fishing

7

Gerry Brady

INTRODUCTION

The period 1949 to 1998 has seen major changes in Irish agriculture. Many of these changes were continuations of longer-term trends, such as the decline in crop areas and numbers of farms and an explosion in livestock numbers. Other changes were driven by policy changes as well as technical and scientific developments. New farmer advisory and farmer representative organisations were established to guide these changes.

Macra na Feirme was formed in 1944 emerging from local agricultural discussion groups. In 1950 the Irish Creamery and Milk Suppliers Association (ICMSA) was formed at Kilmallock in County Limerick, followed in 1954 by the National Farmers Association (NFA), which became the Irish Farmers Association (IFA) in January 1970.

The importance of export markets was recognised with the establishment of an Advisory Committee on the Marketing of Agricultural Produce in May 1957. The series of Reports resulted in a White Paper recommending that an Irish Dairy Produce Board should be set up. In May 1961, An Bord Bainne was established.

With the involvement of the CSO, a Farm Management Survey was started in 1959 by An Foras Talúntais (AFT). The objective was to collect reliable information on farm management and to encourage individual farmers to keep records and accounts. Specially prepared Farm Records and Accounts Books were issued to 220 instructors in agriculture and Parish Agents. The widely used National Farm Survey had its origins here. AFT had been established in 1958 with responsibility for agricultural research. An Chomhairle Oiliúna Talmhaíochta (ACOT) was set up with responsibility for the provision of agricultural advisory and training services. In 1988 Teagasc, the Agriculture and Food Development Authority, was created and AFT, ACOT and the County Committees of Agriculture were dissolved.

LIVESTOCK DISEASES

Although it was a crop disease that was the main cause for initiating the system of agricultural surveys in 1847, cattle diseases have given rise to most concern in the last fifty years. In the autumn of 1951, the danger of a foot and mouth disease outbreak caused the prohibition on the importation of all four-legged animals from Great Britain or continental Europe. A worsening of the situation in 1952 caused an arrangement to be introduced under which every sea and air visitor had to complete a special query card. Every passenger whose card showed that there was a possibility of exposure to infection abroad was required to undergo disinfection before leaving the landing place. The precautions worked, as no outbreak of foot and mouth was recorded between 1941 and 1967.

The bovine tuberculosis eradication scheme was brought into operation in 1954. It was based on voluntary participation by the farming community. The incidence in Ireland at the time was estimated to be 17% in all cattle but appreciably higher in cows. In 1988, ERAD was set up with a target of halving the prevailing incidence of tuberculosis. An intensive testing scheme resulted in some 42 million tests being carried out by 1991, and an estimated 99% of the 7 million cattle in the national herd were free of the disease.

The Disease of Animals (Bovine Spongiform Encephalopathy) Order was introduced in 1989 after the first case of BSE was confirmed on 25 January 1989. In all 15 cases were confirmed that year.

CROPS AND LIVESTOCK

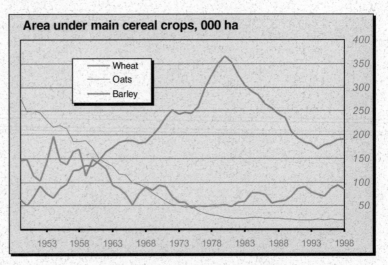

Area under main cereal crops, 000 ha

The area under wheat in 1949 was 147,000 ha. Since then it has declined significantly to 84,000 ha in 1998. The decrease in the area under oats has been much more substantial — from 278,000 in 1949 to 19,000 in 1998. Barley has been an exception with the area rising from 64,000 ha in 1949 to an all-time record of 366,000 ha in 1980. The principal reason for this increase was its use as an animal feedingstuff. However, the area decreased again to 191,000 ha in 1998. Common Agricultural Policy reforms implemented during the 1990s included a compulsory set-aside scheme whereby cereal farmers reduced production by leaving some land unsown in return for financial compensation. Another significant change was the rapid switch from hay to silage during the 1980s and 1990s.

In 1949, the area under potatoes was 142,000 ha but this has since decreased in an almost annual decline to 19,000 ha in 1998.

Farm numbers, crop areas and livestock numbers

Category	1949	1970	1991	1998
Farm holdings (000)	318	280	171†	146
Corn crops (000 ha)	491	381	30	301
Potatoes (000 ha)	142	57	20	19
Cattle (000)	4,127	5,956	6,91	7,795
Sheep (000)	2,192	4,082	8,88	8,373
Poultry (000)	22,077	11,231	12,05	13,147
Horses and Ponies (000)	402	124	63	73

† Some of the decrease between 1970 and 1991 is due to a change in methodology.

Cattle numbers in 1949 were 4.1 million, and they have increased significantly since then, with 1998 numbers reaching 7.8 million. The recent expansion has been in the beef side and has been export-led. Ireland produces 10 times more beef than it needs for the domestic market. Cow numbers have continued to rise, but mainly for beef production because the introduction of milk quotas in the 1980s put a ceiling on milk production.

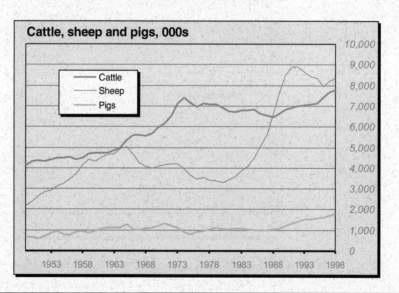

Cattle, sheep and pigs, 000s

The changes in sheep numbers have been more recent and more dramatic. They rose from 2.2 million in 1949 to 5 million in 1965. A period of decline saw them fall to 3.3 million in 1980, but since then the expansion has been visible throughout Ireland, with numbers exceeding cattle in 1988 for the first time since 1901 and almost reaching 9 million in 1992. Environmental concerns, quota ceilings, and lower prices caused some fall in numbers in the 1990s, and a cull of around 140,000 mountain ewes was taken late in 1998.

Poultry numbers in 1930 were 22.9 million. Numbers declined until the late 1940s when a Poultry Development Scheme was established with substantial grants on offer for the establishment and equipment of hatcheries, egg supply farms and pedigree breeding stations. This scheme began the commercialisation of the industry, particularly in the north-east with numbers in Monaghan rising from just under 1 million in 1949 to over 6 million in 1998, or almost a half of total poultry numbers. Similarly, but more recently, the Irish pigmeat industry has become one of the most concentrated in Europe, with 365 farms accounting for over 90% of total pig numbers in December 1997.

Horse and pony numbers were relatively high in 1949 at 402,000. However by 1955 they had fallen to under 300,000 and by 1962 they were under 200,000. In 1974 there were 98,000 recorded and this slowly declined to 59,000 in 1989. In recent years the numbers are rising again as sport, leisure and tourism are stimulating some expansion.

TRENDS IN PRICES AND INCOME

The graph compares trends in the total input and total output price indices, with both series rescaled to 1990 as 100. Both series exhibit a re-

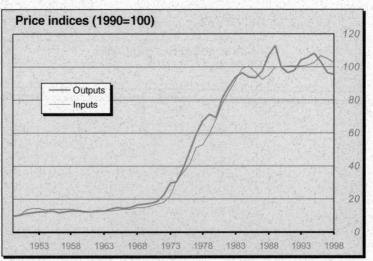

markable stability in prices in the 1949 to 1971 period. Entry to the EEC gave a greater stimulus to output prices and this index generally exceeded the inputs index up to 1995. Since then there has been an annual decline in the output index with the result that the input index is now significantly higher.

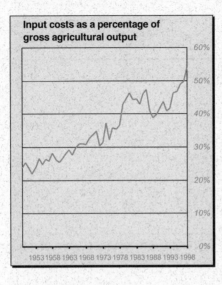

Input costs as a percentage of gross agricultural output

1953 1958 1963 1968 1973 1978 1983 1988 1993 1998

In 1949, the Agriculture industry was underdeveloped, but farm income was derived from a wider base of activities. The cattle and milk sectors accounted for 38% of gross agricultural output. By 1970 this had risen to 54% and now stands at around 67%.

The value of output has increased from £128m in 1949 to £3,270m in 1998. A significant factor has been the change in the cost of inputs — from around 24% of output in 1949 to 54% in 1998, indicating that substantial investment has been necessary and been made by the farming community to increase the output from crops and livestock.

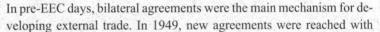

EEC

In pre-EEC days, bilateral agreements were the main mechanism for developing external trade. In 1949, new agreements were reached with

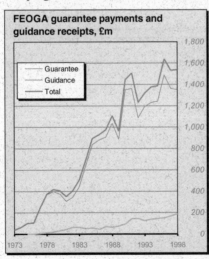

FEOGA guarantee payments and guidance receipts, £m

Guarantee
Guidance
Total

1973　1978　1983　1988　1993　1998

Germany and Sweden. The German agreement was for one year and allowed Ireland to export agricultural and industrial products. The principal items exported to Germany in 1949 were oats (£151,720), butter (£140,000) and cattle (£68,420).

The role of the European Agricultural Guidance and Guarantee Fund (FEOGA) was to meet payments on export refunds for trade to third countries, on compensatory amounts for trade with member states and the costs of intervention. The graph shows the pattern of FEOGA receipts to Ireland since 1973. Around £20 billion has been received between 1973-1998. In the 1990s substantial change was made to the CAP by switching from price guarantees to direct payments. Evidence of the need for such reform was that in 1991, 56% of total beef slaughterings were placed into intervention. International pressure through World trade agreements also acted as a key impetus for CAP reform.

TRENDS IN FORESTRY AND SEA FISHING

After the last ice age, around 10,000 years ago, juniper, willow, birch, hazel, pine, oak, elm, alder and ash gradually began to establish themselves. It was not until the plantation period in the 16th and 17th centuries, when English settlers arrived in large numbers into Ireland, that these natural forests were harvested to provide wood for ships, houses, barrel staves, mining and fuel. Much of the timber was exported to England but it was also used in the mines in Wicklow such as Avoca.

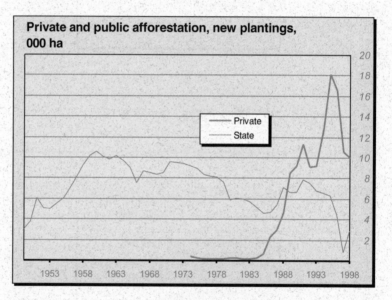

By 1949, forestry in Ireland was relatively underdeveloped. The area of forest land managed by the public sector was 69,000 ha. Since then there has been a considerable increase in both public and private afforestation. Public sector new plantings have risen from below 3,000 ha in 1949 to 8,500 ha in 1970. Since then the public area afforested each year has declined but replanting of felled areas has increased. The most dramatic change in the period has been in the private sector. From little private afforestation up to 1984, the expansion now exceeds the annual public afforested area. Farmers and investment companies were the main parties responsible for these plantings.

While sitka spruce has remained the dominant species, recent planting premia have sought to encourage more broadleaf planting.

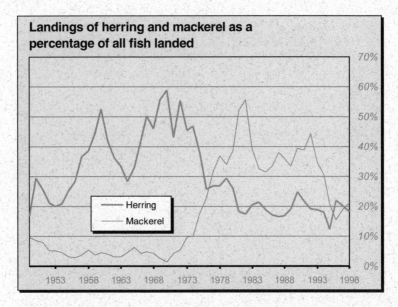

Landings of herring and mackerel as a percentage of all fish landed

An Inland Fisheries Trust was set-up in 1951. This was followed in 1952 by the establishment of An Bord Iascaigh Mhara. Two notable movements are present in the sea landings figures. The total landed weight increased substantially from 12,700 tonnes in 1952 when BIM were established to 376,000 tonnes in 1995. Since then, EU quota restrictions have resulted in a decline in the overall landed weight to around 316,000 tonnes in 1998. The relative proportion each species accounts for has changed due to the combination of quotas and larger, more commercially oriented boats. The graph shows the decreasing relative importance of herring from 59% of the total landed weight in 1970 to around one-fifth in 1998. Conversely, mackerel became very important in the early 1980s, though this has recently been displaced by horse mackerel.

Industry and Construction

8

Tom McMahon

THE AMERICAN UNCLE

In the early 1900s my eldest uncle set out from a small town in West Clare to take the boat from Queenstown and start a new life in America. He was among the thousands of young men and women who had to emigrate in those and later years — hardly a family was left untouched by that experience.

On the road to Limerick, he would have passed close to the marshy wastes of Rineanna close to the river Shannon. He could not have known that by the end of his century an international airport would have sprung up there. Neither could he have dreamt that a cluster of modern factories would have sprung up manufacturing and exporting world-wide products of extraordinary sophistication.

He is long since *ar shlí na fírinne*, but if he were alive today one wonders what he would have made of it all.

His main experience with official statistics would have been the national ritual of the Census of Population. His consumer price index would have been a subjective one based on a sense that inflation was soaring if the price of a bag of tea or his ounce of tobacco rose. He was a man with only basic formal education but his Ireland was a society where learning in general and mathematics in particular were highly valued. He would then, one feels, be fascinated by the thought that by the 1920s his everyday experience of rising prices would be summarised in one number and that people would be summarising in a few numbers the value of what was being manufactured in his country; that by the middle of his century people would methodically summarise using national accounting concepts how his country was developing from year to year; and, finally, that in the later decades governments would nudge the economy this way or that using a mass of economic statistics. Using statistics like that let's have a quick overview of how industry in particular has developed over the last half-century.

During the Second World War, the Emergency affected industrial production. Between 1939 and 1942, output fell by almost a quarter due to the shortage of imported materials. The fall in employment during this period was a more modest 9%. By the late 1940s, the economy was recovering from the effects.

The table shows the extent of change in the transportable goods sector over the last half-century.

Net output has increased over 300-fold from £69m in 1950 to £21,557m in 1997. Most of this is, of course, due to price increases, but even when the price effects are discounted we are still left with a 16-fold increase in real terms over that period.

Changes in industry: Transportable Goods

	Net output at current prices £m	Volume of production 1985=100
1950	69	19
1955	97	23
1960	131	26
1965	222	36
1970	438	51
1975	1,141	58
1980	2,953	78
1985	5,792	100
1990	9,169	148
1997	21,557	299

LIME KILNS.
IN PROCESS OF CONSTRUCTION.

INDUSTRIALISATION

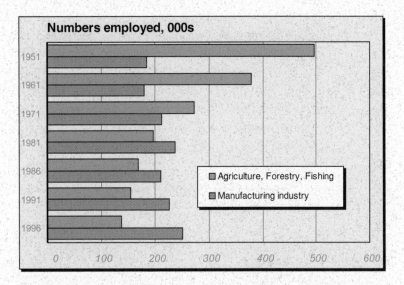

Numbers employed, 000s

The most dramatic change is the change from an agricultural economy to an industrial one. In 1997, manufacturing industry gave rise to more than six times the net output of the agricultural sector. Back in 1949 it was actually less than agricultural output.

There has been a corresponding drop in the numbers engaged in agriculture from 496,000 in 1951 to 138,000 in 1996 and a rise in manufacturing industry from 184,000 in 1951 to 250,000 in 1996.

Net output in manufacturing industries as a multiple of net output in agriculture, forestry and fishing

1949	0.8
1954	1.0
1959	1.1
1964	1.4
1969	2.0
1974	2.2
1979	2.8
1984	3.3
1989	4.0
1994	4.6
1997	6.4

THE CHANGING STRUCTURE OF MANUFACTURING INDUSTRY

Manufacturing industry has also changed enormously within itself. The advance of technology, the increase in the volume of international trade, the greater diversity of Ireland's trade partners, and membership of the EU are some of the factors that have changed the nature of industry.

Nowadays when one thinks of industry in Ireland, the large multinational companies in sectors such as the computer and chemical industries come to mind. Indeed, the major sectors now are the computer sector, both hardware and software, and the pharmaceutical sector. In 1949, the sectors with the highest net output were brewing, bread & flour confectionery, printing & publishing, clothing and sugar & sugar confectionery, which between them accounted for 38% of the total output of transportable goods industry.

The tables show the broad sectors, in terms of their percentage contribution to total transportable goods, that were most important in 1949 and 1997.

Major sectors in 1949

	Share of net output	Share of employment
Brewing	10.7%	3.5%
Bread and flour confectionery	7.5%	7.8%
Clothing	6.9%	12.2%
Sugar and sugar confectionery	6.8%	6.1%
Printing, publishing	6.3%	6.1%

Major sectors in 1997

	Share of net output	Share of employment
Chemicals and pharmaceuticals	28.1%	8.5%
Optical and electrical equipment	18.4%	23.2%
Food products	15.0%	16.5%
Reproduction of computer media and sound recording	11.2%	2.2%

Older readers might recall with nostalgia the sectors considered important by classification experts in 1949. The 27 main sectors used to classify transportable goods included "Linen, cotton, jute and canvas" and "Soap and candles". Lists of what were described as "Principal Products" referred to fellmongery, laces, pigs' heads, pollard and snuff. On the other hand, in the 1940s the first electronic computers were being put through their paces and even they did not yet have the benefit of the newly invented "transistor". Statisticians are often criticised for large changes in nomenclatures in industry, trade and elsewhere, but seeing contrasts such as this reminds one of the dangers of not keeping up with the changing times, even if this sometimes results in breaks in continuity.

In 1949, the largest employing sectors in transportable goods industry were the clothing, bread & flour confectionery, sugar & sugar confectionery and printing & publishing sectors. Between them, they employed about 32% of the total. In 1996, the sectors corresponding roughly to these employed only 14% of the total. On the other hand, the electronics sector was almost non-existent then (the very broad "engineering and implements" sector accounted for only 4% of employment), and even the chemical & drug sector, which accounted for 8% of employment in 1996, accounted for only 1% of employment in 1949.

The regional distribution of industry has also changed. In 1946, about 50% of net output and 41% of employment arose in Dublin city and county. In 1996, the corresponding figures are lower at about 33% for net output and less than 25% for employment. These changes are linked to the development of clusters of industry in areas such as Cork, Limerick, Shannon and Galway, the improved road network (and other infrastructural improvements) throughout the country, and the shifts in population patterns.

ELECTRIC POWER

The expansion in industry over 50 years, along with increased rural electrification and domestic use of electricity, explains the jump in annual electricity output. According to the annual reports of the ESB, output rose from 710 million units in 1949 to 19,651 million units in 1997. During this period, the number of consumers increased more than five-fold from 284,000 to 1,484,000.

The table shows how the pattern of power generation has shifted over the years. The changes reflects the relative costs of different fuels as well as the perceived security of continued supplies of those fuels. The effects of the oil price rises in the 1970s can be observed in the table, though it takes some time for the shifts to occur given the long lead-in times needed for this type of investment.

Sources of electric power
Percentage of gross generation for each type

	1950	1960	1970	1975	1980	1990	1997
Peat	1%	33%	37%	23%	15%	15%	10%
Coal, oil	59%	31%	52%	65%	63%	51%	52%
Gas	–	–	–	–	10%	27%	33%
Hydroelectric and Pumped storage	40%	36%	11%	12%	12%	7%	5%
Total	100%	100%	100%	100%	100%	100%	100%

INCREASED OUTPUT

While the value of transportable goods production rose between 1950 and 1997 over 300-fold, the truer underlying picture is that the overall volume increased by a factor of about 16.

During the last fifty years, the growth of industry has been affected by some economic milestones. These can arise from planned policies or initiatives or from unexpected events. Ones which come to mind are the Programmes for Economic Expansion, particularly the first one in 1961, the Anglo-Irish trade agreement in 1966, the entry into the EEC in 1973, EMS entry in 1978, and the completion of the internal market and the dropping of intra-EU Customs controls in 1993. Unplanned events include the oil price rises of 1973 and 1979.

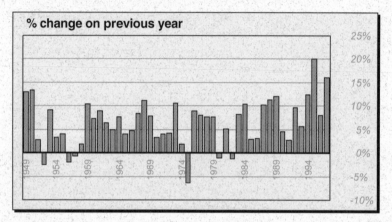

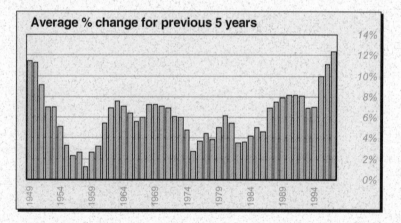

The two graphs try to illustrate the effect, if any, on industrial growth of such milestones, and readers are invited to draw their own conclusions from them. The first shows the annual percentage change and the second shows the average over the previous five years.

Of course, milestones like this are never the full reason for change. Ongoing government policy decisions, the international economic climate, and the work of development agencies will have an effect on the growth rate. Nevertheless, the effects of these milestones seem clear in a number of cases. This is particularly the case with the oil price rises, where the downturn is very evident. Of course, this would also have been caused by the international recessions caused by these events.

During the period the average numbers engaged in transportable goods industries covered by the Census of Industrial Production rose from 144 thousand in 1950 to 246 thousand in 1997. This leads to roughly a 9-fold increase in the volume of production per person.

INDUSTRIAL EARNINGS

In 1949, the average weekly adult earnings in the transportable goods sector were £5.59 for males and £2.97 for females. In 1998, the averages were £331.87 and £218.96 respectively. If you take into account the increase in the consumer price index in the period (by a factor of 21), male earnings have almost trebled and female earnings have more than trebled in the period.

Average weekly earnings

	1949	1959	1969
Male	£5.59	£9.11	£20.70
Female	£2.97	£4.93	£9.76
Female earnings as a % of male	53%	54%	47%

	1979	1989	1998
Male	£100.55	£250.63	£331.87
Female	£58.09	£152.50	£218.96
Female earnings as a % of male	58%	61%	66%

The number of hours worked at 46.2 for males and 43.9 for females in 1949 was higher than the present levels, which is not surprising when one considers the perceived increase in leisure time.

Average weekly hours worked

	1949	1959	1969	1979	1989	1998
Male	46.2	46.9	45.5	44.2	43.6	41.9
Female	43.9	43.5	39.4	38.3	38.3	37.5

In 1949, the highest male earners were in the tobacco sector followed by the brewing sector. In 1997, the sectors corresponding to these, as well some of the chemicals subsectors, tended to have the highest weekly earnings. Among females, the highest earners were also in the tobacco sector.

The difference in average weekly earnings between males and females, while less than in 1949, is still very noticeable. It seems likely that the factors that explain the difference today are much the same as 50 years ago, such as lesser length of service, less availing of overtime, and more part-time working on the part of women. One factor, which was no doubt present then but not now, was the practice of paying women a somewhat lower rate for similar work.

SIZE OF FIRMS

The table shows how the average size of industrial firms has changed. The shift in size category over the years has been a gradual one with a slightly larger percentage of firms being in the larger size categories in 1996 than was the case in 1949. It is still the case though that most firms have fewer than twenty persons engaged.

Percentage of firms in each size category (Transportable goods industries)

Persons engaged	1949	1979	1996
Less than 20	60.7%	57.2%	54.3%
20-49	21.2%	21.0%	23.6%
50 or more	18.1%	21.8%	22.1%
Total	100.0%	100.0%	100.0%

NATIONALITY OF FIRMS

Nationality data were first collected for 1983, and the table shows the trend since then. While the proportion of Irish-owned firms remained almost unchanged, there was a gradual decline in their share of employment from 60.9% in 1983 to 53.0% in 1996.

Nationality of firms

	Firms			Persons		
	Irish	Foreign	Total	Irish	Foreign	Total
1983	83.1%	16.9%	100.0%	60.9%	39.1%	100.0%
1987	83.2%	16.8%	100.0%	57.2%	42.8%	100.0%
1991	83.6%	16.4%	100.0%	55.9%	44.1%	100.0%
1995	84.3%	15.7%	100.0%	52.9%	47.1%	100.0%
1996	84.1%	15.9%	100.0%	53.0%	47.0%	100.0%

THE CONSTRUCTION INDUSTRY

The construction industry has always been one of the most important sectors from the point of view of employment. By early 1999, about 149,000 persons in employment were classified to the construction sector.

Average earnings in the sector reflect the general change in wage levels. In 1949, average weekly earnings for adult males in the sector were £5.95. At the end of 1998 average weekly earnings ranged from £213.41 for apprentices to £480.63 for foremen.

There has been a large increase in housebuilding. The successive censuses of population show that there has been an increase of 52% in the number of private dwellings between the 1946 and 1991 censuses. The population increased by only 19% in the same period, so the trend towards fewer persons living in an average dwelling, for whatever reason, is obvious here.

Permanent private housing units

	Number
1946	663,000
1961	676,000
1971	705,000
1981	876,000
1991	1,007,000

A topic of burning interest both then and now is house prices. Unfortunately, reliable data are not available from fifty years ago. However, over the last thirty years or so, the Department of the Environment have been publishing average new house prices for which loans had been approved. An index of prices derived from data such as these is not a perfect measure of how the underlying price of a house changes over the years. The quality of new houses being built changes from year to year. For example, the average floor size and site size may get smaller but there may be more extras like central heating or double-glazing. It is also very difficult to quantify the effect of location on price. Nonetheless, the series is still useful as a very broad indicator of how house prices have changed.

Average prices of new houses (for which loans were approved)

	Dublin	Cork	All
1968	£4,500	£3,800	£4,200
1973	£7,100	£6,400	£7,100
1978	£20,300	£17,700	£19,000
1983	£37,900	£30,900	£35,000
1988	£45,700	£39,100	£41,300
1993	£59,500	£53,700	£55,000
1998	£124,200	£87,700	£97,800

A comparison with the trend in the consumer price index is shown in the table for all areas and in the graph for Dublin and Cork. (The outright purchase of dwellings is not covered in the CPI as it is regarded as a capital investment. However, mortgage interest cost is included in the index and this reflects the prices of new dwellings.)

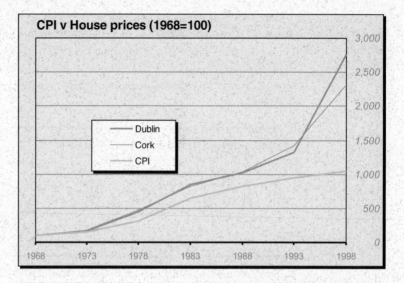

CPI v House prices (1968=100)

Comparison of new house prices with CPI (1968=100)

	House price index	CPI
1968	100.0	100.0
1973	167.5	153.2
1978	447.7	312.6
1983	826.4	652.0
1988	975.2	816.4
1993	1299.3	947.4
1998	2309.6	1050.3

CONCLUSION

And how would the American uncle have reacted? There would have been pride that his country of birth had gone from being a struggling economy to one at the cutting edge of technology. There would have been a vigorous nod of approval at the change in attitude from weary resignation to one that said that few things were impossible. But perhaps what would have pleased him most is that, unlike him, so many of the young people who still emigrate do so not out of necessity but by choice. Perhaps they do so out of a sense of adventure, perhaps as part of a career plan to gain experience and then return and maybe even set up a new company in Ireland. Whatever the reason, many of them now emigrate with qualifications and skills which make them world-beaters.

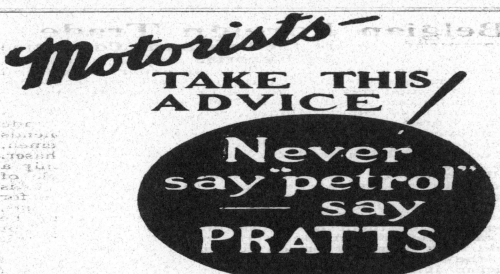

MODERN OFFICE

Copying by Copycat!

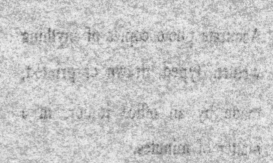

Accurate clean copies of anything
drawn, typed, written or printed,
made by an office machine, in a
matter of minutes.

One operator and a cover
can equal the type top of or
three copy press and therein
is used for checking copies.

Copycat has about four places
copying to most of the
surgical office or starting
other tasks.

The Services Sector

Joe Madden

INTRODUCTION

O n the verge of the 21st century, the Irish economy has, in line with developments elsewhere in Europe, become largely a service economy. A service economy is sometimes characterised as post-industrial and is difficult to define precisely. The sector encompasses a vast and varied grouping of economic activities and can broadly be regarded as all the residual sectors of the economy excluding the Agriculture, Industry and Construction sectors.

More precisely, the services sectors are:

- Distributive trade

- Hotels and restaurants

- Transport, storage and communication

- Financial intermediation

- Real estate, renting and business activities

- Public administration

- Education; health and social work

- Other community, social and personal services.

It is clear, therefore, that the services sector as defined above is quite extensive, but even this is not the full story since manufacturing activities, for example, may produce both goods and services (such as after-sales service) with the output of the "service activity" being included with the manufacturing output. The services sector has been monitored by the CSO to a varying degree since 1933 when the first Census of Distribution took place, but increasingly so since 1988 when a detailed Census of Services was carried out.

INCREASING IMPORTANCE OF THE SERVICES SECTOR

The table and graph show the contribution to total employment made by the three broad sectors of the economy for 1926 to 1996. Agriculture includes Forestry and Fishing, and Industry includes Mining and Construction.

Sectoral employment (000)

	Agriculture	Industry	Services	Total
1926	654	158	410	1,222
1951	496	282	439	1,217
1971	273	323	459	1,055
1981	189	366	583	1,138
1991	158	313	678	1,149
1996	134	354	819	1,307

Sectoral employment (%)

	Agriculture	Industry	Services	Total
1926	53	13	34	100
1951	41	23	36	100
1971	26	31	43	100
1981	17	32	51	100
1991	14	27	59	100
1996	10	27	63	100

There has been a dramatic shift from Agriculture to Services: while the numbers at work in Industry changed relatively little, the numbers in Agriculture declined by a factor of 4 and the numbers in Services almost doubled. During the lifetime of the CSO, the importance of the services sector to the economy in terms of employment has almost doubled, with the sector now employing about two-thirds of all jobs. The tables and graph show a pattern of employment that is typical of developing countries in the 20th century: a steady decline in employment in Agriculture, an increase in Industrial employment in the earlier period, and an increase in services employment in the latest period.

The importance of the sector is observed not only in terms of employment but also in terms of output as measured by its contribution to GDP.

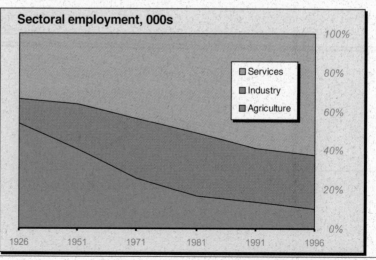

Sectoral employment, 000s

The table below illustrates the increasing importance of the sector in terms of national productivity.

Contribution of Services to GDP

	Services GDP £m	Total GDP £m	Services as a % of GDP
1949	135	330	41%
1960	255	563	45%
1970	687	1,420	48%
1975	1,702	3,505	49%
1980	4,746	8,918	53%
1985	9,228	17,398	53%
1990	14,258	25,347	56%
1995	20,487	36,709	56%
1997	25,282	44,723	57%

The services sector now dominates the Irish economy by contributing about two-thirds of both the employment and wealth created. Statistics for the European economy as a whole yield a somewhat similar but not so stark picture, with the services contribution being about a half of the total.

DEVELOPMENT OF SERVICES STATISTICS IN IRELAND

The first Census of Distribution in Ireland was undertaken in respect of the year 1933. It was a pioneering exercise at the time and was reputed to be the first such inquiry in Europe. It was prompted by a need to collect comprehensive statistics on a part of the economy — the distribution of goods — which was growing in importance and which was not hitherto covered by official inquiries. The data were recorded on punched cards and compiled using sorting and counting machinery.

The total number of shops included in the Census was 46,000. Many were very small: half had turnovers of less than £500 per annum, and 14% had turnovers of under £100. (£100 in 1933 is worth about as much as £4,500 now.) Of the total, 1,788 were classified as "Hucksters", a type of very small family run shop, two-thirds of which had turnovers of less than £100. The highest level of retail sales per head of the population was in Dublin at £115 per annum. On the other hand, sales of £30 per head or less were recorded in shops in Leitrim, Clare, Kerry South and Mayo West.

Further censuses of distribution were taken in respect of the years 1951, 1956, 1966, 1971 and 1977. In addition to retail and wholesale trade, some of these censuses covered a limited number of other services. However, the 1988 Census was the first to cover all service activities with the exception of financial services and the public sector. The only other major sources of services information in Ireland, historically, had been the Censuses of Population, which gave detailed employment statistics from 1926 and more recently the monthly Retail Sales Index, first published in 1962. In more recent years, the importance of the service sector has led to a considerable expansion in the range and frequency of the statistics available on the sector.

CHANGES SINCE 1951

The table gives a summary of the relative importance of outlet types according to the legal status of ownership in 1951 and 1999. There has been a significant shift from the smaller proprietor or partnerships to private limited companies. Moreover, a much greater share of turnover is attributable to private limited companies at the expense of the smaller operators.

Retail outlets: Legal status of ownership

Legal status	1951	1999
Individual proprietorship or partnership	93.3%	65.6%
Private limited company	5.4%	31.1%
Public limited company	0.8%	0.6%
Co-operative society and others	0.5%	2.7%
Total	100.0%	100.0%

The number of retail outlets classified by employment size class for the years 1951 and 1999 is given in the table. The proportion of retail sales accounted for by each size class in 1991 and 1997 is also shown.

Retail outlets: Employment size

Numbers engaged	Number of retail outlets		Total retail sales	
	1951	1999	1951	1997
1	25.6%	24.8%	3.1%	2.3%
2	28.0%	27.8%	8.3%	4.3%
3	17.1%	15.4%	10.0%	5.1%
4	10.6%	9.8%	9.5%	5.6%
5-9	14.1%	14.5%	26.7%	17.3%
10-14	2.4%	3.0%	10.9%	8.7%
15-19	0.9%	1.0%	5.8%	6.6%
20-49	1.0%	1.6%	12.5%	17.9%
50 & over	0.3%	2.0%	13.2%	32.2%
Total	100.0%	100.0%	100.0%	100.0%

The table shows that there was an increased percentage of sales attributable to the larger outlets in 1997 by comparison with 1951.

The level of retail sales per head of population increased from £67 in 1951 to £3,852 in 1996. When the effect of inflation is discounted, this suggests a "real" increase in the volume or quantity of sales of about 310%. In 1951, sales per establishment were £6,618 and sales per person employed were £1,833. The corresponding figures for 1996 were £322,100 and £75,800. These figures suggest volume changes of about 260% and 220% respectively. In 1951, outlets with 5-9 persons engaged contributed the highest proportion of total sales at 26.7%, whereas in 1997, outlets with 50 or more persons engaged contributed the highest proportion of total sales at 32.2%.

Wages and salaries per person were £224 in 1951. In 1996, the figure had risen to about £8,600, suggesting a volume or "real" increase of about 210%. In 1951, the highest paid employees were in "Coal, turf and other solid fuels", with £361 per annum whereas the lowest paid were in "Tobacco, sweets and newspapers" with £155 per annum. In 1996, the highest paid employees were in "Motor trades" with £10,655 per annum whereas the lowest paid were in "Specialised store sales of food, beverages and tobacco" with £6,304 per annum.

EMPLOYMENT IN SERVICES

The graphs compare 1951 sectoral employment with that of 1997. The most striking structural change in the employment figures occurred in female employment. The proportion of female employment in the Personal Services sector fell from 37% in 1951 to 17% in 1997. On the other hand, the proportion of females employed in professional services

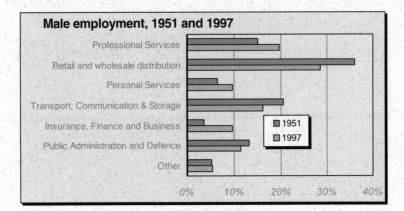

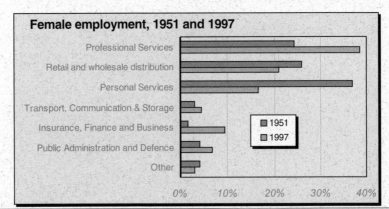

rose from 24% in 1951 to 38% in 1997. Another notable sectoral rise occurred in the Insurance, Finance and Business services sector.

The sectoral employment in the service sectors for the year 1997 is given in the table below.

Sectoral employment in the services sector, 1997 (000)

	Males	Females	Total
Professional services	80	158	238
Retail and wholesale distribution	116	86	203
Personal services	39	68	107
Transport, communication & storage	66	18	84
Insurance, finance and business	39	39	78
Public administration and defence	46	28	74
Other	22	13	34
Total	408	410	818

It is particularly interesting to note from the table that, whereas equal numbers of males and females are employed in the Insurance, finance and business sector, twice as many females as males are employed in Professional services.

In conclusion, it appears that the services sector will continue to expand into the new millennium, providing further increased employment and output. From a statistical point of view, this continued expansion will demand ever-increasing attention from statisticians in their quest to understand developments in the economy.

"THAT'S RIGHT, MAC.

I changed over to E.S.B. supply about three years ago . . .
Well, I'm satisfied any way . . . No—running your own
power plant is not cheap—just eats up money when you reckon
in everything . . . You'll be making no mistake if you change
over. It was the best move I ever made. What with
increased work and the new machinery we've put in I
couldn't possibly have carried on otherwise for the past two
years . . . Cost? Well, the figure I go on is my
production cost and that's gone down very considerably . . .
Call over some time and I'll show you round . . . "

7 DIFFERENT CHASSIS
50 STANDARD BODY MODELS

There's a Bedford to suit *your* loads

8-cwt. chassis £158   Van £210

12-cwt. chassis £177   Van £232

30-cwt. chassis £210   Lorry £264

2-ton short chassis £228
2-ton long chassis £240 Lorry £297

3-ton short chassis £278
3-ton long chassis £294 Lorry £369

Tourism and Transport

Maureen Delamere

10

TOURISM

Tourism in Ireland has shown unprecedented growth over the past 50 years and has undergone a complete metamorphosis. It was severely affected during and after the war. It was estimated that receipts from tourism and travel amounted to a relatively modest £18m in 1946. Earnings from overseas visitors passed the £1 billion level in 1990, and just 8 years later it had more than doubled to £2.3 billion.

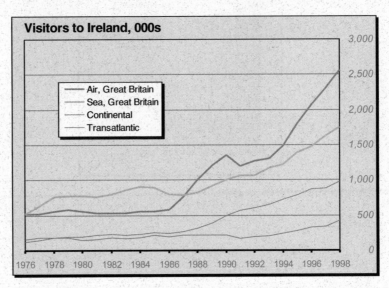

The most dramatic changes in tourist numbers occurred in recent years. The total number of visitors to Ireland passed three million in 1990. In fact, the targeting of tourism from a policy perspective is fairly recent, dating back principally to the Programme for National Recovery (1987). This identified tourism as an area of considerable potential, and a commitment was given to its development. It was preceded by a proposed package of measures presented by the council in 1980 (NESC Report No. 52, *Tourism Policy*) designed to produce a more focused approach to marketing, promotion and industry training, and to deal with problems created by seasonality.

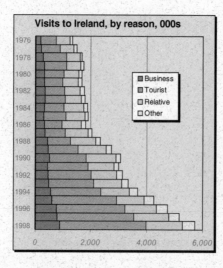

Visits to Ireland, by reason, 000s

Between 1990 and 1998, the number of visitors to Ireland almost doubled to 5.7 million. Its growth in recent years is attributable to a variety of factors, notably the impact of low inflation and a stable exchange rate within the EMS on our competitiveness as a holiday location, liberalisation of air transport, and a substantial growth in visitor numbers from continental Europe, reflecting improved marketing.

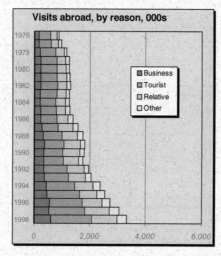

Visits abroad, by reason, 000s

Over the six-year period to 1992, an increase in overseas tourism of 1.3 million was recorded, indicating a compound growth rate of 9.5% per annum. As always, most of the visitors come from the UK, and in absolute terms most of the increase was from the UK. However, the biggest relative increase was for visitors from continental Europe. In 1976, there were only 123,000 visitors from continental Europe. By 1992, however, Britain's share had fallen to 56% and continental Europe, now supplying 27% of visits, had pushed North America into third place at 13%. There was a more recent surge in the number of North American visitors, in the five-year period 1993-1998, when the numbers more than doubled to pass 850,000.

The numbers of Irish people travelling abroad has also been rising strongly. It passed the two million level in 1993, and five years later, by 1998, it reached 3,330,000. Growth in outbound tourism is therefore averaging at around 10% per annum.

The first graph gives an analysis of the reasons why people visit Ireland. It shows that, while all categories show an increase, the bulk of the increase was for tourists. The second graph, on the same scale, shows why Irish people travel abroad.

RAIL AND CANAL TRANSPORT

In Ireland — an island economy on the edge of Europe which has to overcome geographic obstacles before reaching its markets — the efficiency of the transport sector is absolutely crucial. Any deficiencies in our transport network add to the cost of exports and imports and undermine Ireland's attraction as a location for industry. In line with these demands, the transport sector in Ireland has evolved and expanded enormously over the past 50 years.

Ireland's first steam-powered railway — the Dublin to Kingstown (now Dún Laoghaire) — was opened in 1834, only three years after the first passenger railway in the world, the Liverpool to Manchester line. Despite this early start, railways were slow to develop in Ireland. By 1845, some 2,200 miles of railways had been built in Britain but only 65 to 70 miles of railway were then in use in Ireland, operating on short routes radiating mainly from Dublin and Belfast.

In 1949, Córas Iompair Éireann (CIE) operated most of the railway line in the country, while other companies operated the railways that were situated partly in Northern Ireland. The most notable of these was the Great Northern, but there was a number of smaller companies, such as the Dundalk, Newry and Greenore Railway (which ceased to operate in December 1951), and the Lough Swilly Railway (which ceased in August 1953). The total number of persons engaged in these companies in 1949 was almost 3,000. By comparison, there were 4,900 persons engaged in Irish Rail in 1997.

Railways came under severe pressure from road transport from the early 1920s onwards. Before the Second World War, a tribunal of enquiry was established to investigate public transport, proposing to close down three-eighths of the system. The situation was temporarily relieved by the outbreak of the Second World War. Reduction in fuel supplies diverted both passengers and goods in the private transport sector over to public transport. However, after the War, closures were inevitable. In 1949, a total of 3,675 miles of railway lines were open to traffic compared with 2,953 ten years later, 1,935 in 1970, and 1,758 in 1997.

Notwithstanding this and the heavy increase in freight carried by road, much freight is still carried by rail. For example, in 1949, the two main railway companies transported 211,000 tons of ale and porter; the corresponding amount transported by Irish Rail in 1997 was 274,000 tonnes. The tonnage of beet pulp carried rose from 29,000 to 163,000 tonnes in the same period.

The Grand and Royal canals provided horse-drawn services for passengers and goods between Dublin and Shannon from the end of the eighteenth century. Passenger canal transport disappeared in the early 1850s with the advent of road coaches and cars travelling cross-country routes and providing services between main railway lines and towns. In 1949, a total of 143,000 tons of traffic was carried over the Grand Canal (208 miles) and the Royal Canal (96 miles). This includes 2,200 tons of coal, coke, turf and patent fuel, 4,600 tons of building materials, 102,000 tons of agricultural produce and 34,000 tons of other goods.

SEA TRANSPORT

For an island that had depended for so long on sailing vessels for contact with Britain and the Continent, the advent of steam shipping was of great importance. The first cross-channel steamer started to operate on the Howth-Holyhead route in 1819. By 1826, the new City of Dublin Steam Packet Company operated fourteen vessels, these vessels attaining world record speeds of 24 knots by the end of the nineteenth century. An Irish-owned vessel, the Sirius, made the first transatlantic steam-powered crossing in 1838. In spite of this and attempts to develop Galway as a terminus for transatlantic steamship services, Ireland was effectively out of the transatlantic race by 1850. However, until the demise of transatlantic passenger steamship services because of air competition, Cobh was a frequent stopping point for many transatlantic liners.

For many decades, steamships operated on the main routes between Ireland and Britain. Later, the number of routes and services declined and for much of the second half of the twentieth century, there were virtually no daytime services. In 1949, there were 78 steam vessels registered (under the Merchant Shipping Act, 1894) but only one in 1996 (under the Merchant Shipping Act, 1894 and Mercantile Marine Act, 1955).

The "mail-boats" (operated under a contract with the Post Office) survived the post-war transfer of the first-class mail contract to air transport, and disappeared only with the much later advent of the car ferries on the Dún Laoghaire-Holyhead route. With the introduction of car ferries on a number of routes over thirty years ago, sea transport came into its own. Today, one quarter of traffic between Ireland and Britain still moves by sea. In 1949, there were 324 motor vessels registered compared with 1802 in 1996.

In fact, sea-borne trade is a barometer of economic prosperity and is a vital interconnection in the transport chain: more than 95% of Irish exports go through our ports. The amount of cargo handled at Irish ports increased by nearly 50% in the six-year period 1992-1998.

In 1949, 8,085 vessels with 7,719,000 tons arrived In Ireland, of which 5,550 were steam vessels with 5,185,000 tons in cargoes and ballast. This compares with 16,669 vessels in 1998 carrying 28,694,000 tonnes.

There has been continued significant growth in the number of ferry passengers at the four key roll-on/roll-off passenger ports of Dublin, Dún Laoghaire, Rosslare and Ringaskiddy. The table compares passenger movements by sea for 1949 and 1998, distinguishing Great Britain from other areas.

Passenger Movements (000)

	Great Britain		Other places		Total	
	Outward	Inward	Outward	Inward	Outward	Inward
1949	638	626	15	11	653	637
1998	2,290	2,306	131	128	2,421	2,434

AIR TRANSPORT

As an island, Ireland might have been expected to be a natural focus for air transport. However, despite the initiation of civil air transport in 1919, it was only in 1933 that the first air service to and from Ireland was launched. It operated a Dublin-Belfast route as well as one from Liverpool to Dublin. Aer Lingus operated the first Irish-owned air services in May 1936, from Dublin to Bristol (later extended to London) as well as to the Isle of Man and Liverpool. Aer Lingus launched the first Irish transatlantic service in 1948.

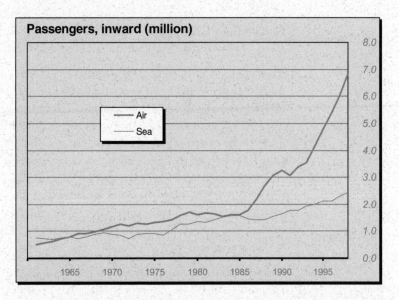

The liberalisation of air transport by the Irish and British Governments from the mid-1980s onwards led to intense competition. This resulted in an enormous increase in cross-channel traffic between Ireland and Britain. In fact, air cross-channel traffic doubled in the period 1984-1988, and more than doubled again in the ten-year period 1988-1998.

In 1949, there were 17,000 flights in and out of Dublin airport carrying 213,000 passengers, compared with 162,000 flights in 1998 carrying 10,787,000 passengers. The table compares the numbers of cross-channel passengers to or from Dublin in 1950 and 1998, and shows in particular the dramatic increase on the Dublin-London routes.

Cross-channel flights

Route	1950	1998
Dublin-London	106,000	4,071,000
Dublin-Liverpool	26,000	170,000
Dublin-Shannon	10,000	148,000
Dublin-Glasgow	25,000	396,000
Dublin-Manchester	24,000	632,000
Dublin-Jersey	1,000	14,000
Dublin-Isle of Man	8,000	41,000
Dublin-Birmingham	11,000	611,000
Total	211,000	6,083,000

The graph of inward passenger flows shows that, while there was a dramatic increase in recent years in passengers arriving by air, it was not at the expense of sea transport.

ROAD TRANSPORT

In 1949, a Ford Anglia (8 horsepower) cost £309 plus import tax while a Ford Prefect (10 horsepower) cost £350. By comparison, in 1999, a Ford Ka costs £8,910 and a Ford Fiesta Encore costs £10,210 (Source: SIMI).

Road transport and freight services were slow to develop in Ireland. This was partly due to the disturbed political climate in the years from 1916 onwards, but also due to the deficiencies in the road network. However, from the 1920s onwards, road transport began to come into its own, putting both the railways and city tramway systems under severe pressure. During the late 1920s, many private bus operations began in Dublin city. Horse trams operated in Cork (originally also in Galway but they were replaced by buses in 1919). Buses replaced the horse-trams in Cork in 1931. From 1938, double-deck buses replaced trams in Dublin. This process was temporarily halted by the onset of the Second World War but was completed in 1949.

The war-related reduction of fuel supplies also hit the private transport sector, diverting both passengers and goods to public transport, whose services had to be curtailed, thus ensuring a very high utilisation of available capacity. The fuel shortages resulted in very few new cars being registered and licensed during and shortly after the war, though by 1947 a recovery was well under way: The number of new cars registered in 1945 was only 261, but four years later it had risen to over 15,000.

The closure of railway lines after the War stimulated further growth of private car ownership. In 1949, 45.4 million gallons of fuel were imported for home use, an increase of almost five-fold on 1944, just five years previous. Under the 1948 Finance Act, the price of petrol was fixed in the range 2s. 9d. to 2s. 10d. per gallon with duty of 1s. 2d. during the period 1948-1951. There was an increase of about 40% in the number of private cars in 1956 compared with 1951.

By 1968, the number of private cars licensed had increased to 348,000. In 1996, it reached the one million mark and only two years later it had risen to 1.2 million.

New private cars licensed initially peaked in 1973 at 75,000 but dropped off until a new record was set in 1977. There was a dramatic surge the following year when 106,000 new cars were licensed. The 100,000 barrier was again breached in 1981, but it was to be another 15 years before this was to happen again: 109,000 new cars were licensed in 1996. There were further big increases in the next two years, and in 1998, a total of 139,000 new cars were licensed.

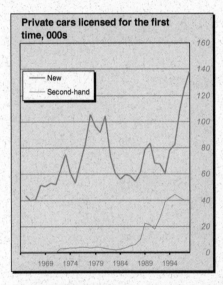

There were 213 fatalities on our roads in 1949, of which only 15 were car users, the bulk of the remainder being pedestrians and pedal cyclists. With the increase of motorisation on the roads, fatalities also rose, peaking in 1972 when 640 people died on the roads. However, the number of road deaths, while still high, has decreased a lot since then: in 1997, there were 472 fatalities, of which 130

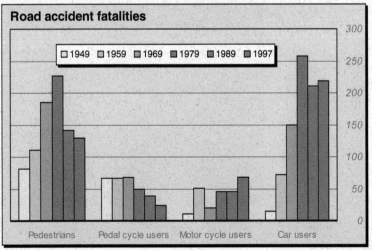

were pedestrians, 219 were car users and 24 were pedal cyclists.

CONCLUSION

Tourism and transport infrastructure has developed and expanded enormously over the last century. However, the period of really intense development has been over the past fifty years, in line with economic, demographic and social demands. We, indeed, have come a long way from when the mail-boats were winning acclaim for attaining world record speeds of 24 knots before the end of the nineteenth century.

Photo Captions

1. Corpus Christi Procession

2. Milk Rationing

3. Child Minding

4. Shop Front

5. Cargo Handling

6. Textiles Industry

7. Harvesting Wheat

8. Road-laying

9. Fair Day

10. Travelling by Steam

Credits

The photographs were supplied courtesy of The Examiner Newspaper and date from the 1940s and 1950s.

The historic advertisements, most of which date from the 1940s, are included solely for the purposes of illustration and are taken from the historic issues of the quarterly *Irish Trade Journal and Statistical Bulletin*, the precursor of the CSO's current *Statistical Bulletin*.